The Womb of Advent

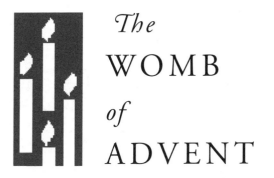

The
WOMB
of
ADVENT

MARK BOZZUTI-JONES

CHURCH PUBLISHING
an imprint of
Church Publishing Incorporated, New York

Quotations from the Bible are from the *New Revised Standard Version.*
© 1989 by the Division of Christian Education of the National Council
of the Churches of Christ in the U.S.A. Used by permission.

Library of Congress Cataloging-in-Publication Data
Bozzuti-Jones, Mark Francisco, 1966–
The Womb of Advent / Mark Bozzuti-Jones.
     p.   cm.
ISBN 978-0-89869-567-0 (pbk.)
1. Advent. I. Title.
BV40.B69 2007
242'.332—dc22   2007014655

Printed in the United States of America.

Church Publishing, Incorporated
445 Fifth Avenue
New York, New York 10016

5   4   3   2   1

Christ is coming, prepare the way.
Christ has come, live the way.
Christ will come again, live lives worthy of his coming.

CONTENTS

Acknowledgments / ix
Preface: In the Beginning / xi

The First Week of Advent
   God's Creation 1

The Second Week of Advent
   God Announces Life and Birth 27

The Third Week of Advent
   Our Call from God 52

The Fourth Week of Advent
   Good News and Light 83

Christmas Day
   The Feast of the Incarnation 112

ACKNOWLEDGMENTS

This book began as a response to all that led up to the birth of our son, Mark Anthony. Kathy, my wife, had had two very difficult pregnancies and we just about thought that there was no hope for us to have a child. The Rev. Jonathan Appleyard, a priest in the Diocese of Maine and a dear friend of mine, encouraged me to pray that the love with which God holds me and with which I hold Kathy "would empower her womb to hold onto my seed." That started my thinking about the womb as not just a place of gestation, but a home, a place where so much can go wrong and where so many wonderful things occur.

Soon after that, Kathy got pregnant and we rejoiced. Twenty weeks later, she underwent a cervical cerclage because the baby was pushing out of the womb too early, and Kathy had to be on bedrest for the rest of the pregnancy. During those months we had regular visits to the doctors and many ultrasound pictures.

The images of our unborn son made me think of myself in the womb, and when Advent and Christmas came I could not help but think of Jesus in the womb. I searched for a book with which I could pray and was surprised that none existed quite in the way I had imagined it. So I decided to write it.

No one saw this book or heard about it until Ken Arnold, then head of Church Publishing, expressed an interest. I thank him for helping to bring it to birth. Cynthia Shattuck became my editor—so, like Jesus, this book had both a mother and a father editor as midwife.

I also want to acknowledge all single parents, teenage mothers, and all who have children outside our traditional understanding of the family. May this book be for you who read it a wonderful way to anticipate and celebrate life, birth, Advent, and Christmas.

Preface

IN THE
BEGINNING

Advent celebrates the gestation of Christ, while Christmas focuses on the nativity of Christ.

Advent stands at the beginning of the church's liturgical year, a time for all Christians to prepare for the birth of our Savior, the Child Christ. During this time of preparation, we seek to place our lives next to the events of Bethlehem, knowing that in Christ we are reborn and claimed as God's own forever.

The whole of Christmas and the salvation story is premised on the birth of the Child—it is how we get to know the Child, through his birth. The birth of the Child offers us a glimpse and hope of new life, and yet during Advent we have often failed to pay sufficient attention to the Child in the womb.

During these four weeks, we seek to be born anew and to proclaim in word and deed the possibility of new life for all humanity. By the time Christians begin the season of Advent, the commercial world has already declared it's Christmas. With the materialism surrounding the celebration Christmas, we sometimes forget that Advent is primarily a season of penitential waiting and reflection—with a heavy dose of joyful expectation. With happy hearts we are invited to renew our faith, fast, deepen our prayer life, and prepare ourselves for the coming of Christ.

Now more than ever, we who love the Child Christ must remind our brothers and sisters that the reason for the season is the incarnation of Christ—the Word who "was made flesh and dwelt among us" or "pitched his tent among us"—while remembering the promise of Jesus to return in glory.

To reflect on the historical birth of the Child and to await his coming has no value unless we nurture the birth of this Child in our hearts and world every day. Celebrating his birth invites us to participate in actions that help in the fulfillment of God's mission to bring good news to the poor, to release the captives and all who are oppressed, and to proclaim the year of the Lord's favor (Luke 4:18–19).

In Scripture, the accounts of Jesus' birth vary from no account in Mark and John to a drama-laden series of events in Matthew and Luke. Matthew and Luke beautifully weave a birth story that involves a whole host of characters who respond differently to the birth of Christ. Gabriel, Mary, Joseph, the angels, the shepherds, the magi, Herod, Anna, and Simeon reflect our present-day celebration of Christmas. In all of these characters we can see how different human beings respond *uniquely* to the good news of Christ.

These liturgical readings for Advent, I strongly believe, are as much about *our* birth as they are about Jesus' birth. They are about our identification with the events we read or hear in Scripture. An often neglected response to the readings of the season of Advent is to recognize how much we are like the Child in his birth. It is the one thing in Jesus' life that all human beings can identify with in a personal way: the Child was in the womb of his mother and was born. We lived in our mother's womb, and so did Jesus.

As we anticipate the birth of Jesus, we see the power and grace in his development in the womb as much as in his nativity. During the four weeks before his birth, the time we celebrate today as Advent, Jesus' body was undergoing changes and adjustments for birth.

It is not just the feast of Christmas that is built upon a birth; in truth, the whole of Christianity stands on this fact that a Child was born for us. Everything began with a birth, and yet we pay little attention to its reality: the surprise, pain, and physical discomfort Mary must have experienced; the blood and the trauma of birth; the fetal development that Jesus must necessarily have known. When we ignore this reality, we lose a sense of the divine. Without entering into debates about when life in the womb begins, we can at least hold to this truth: Jesus was alive in his mother's womb and entered the world as a sign of God as the God of life.

Nothing is more miraculous, frightening, tenuous, painful, physical, and mysterious than birth. Yet we rob ourselves of tremendous opportunities for growth and grace when we jump too easily to Jesus' birth and pay little attention to the months he lived in Mary's womb.

Modern-day science allows us to know a lot more about how an infant develops in the womb, and yet even with all our knowledge, much of what happens is still a mystery. Our knowledge of the child before birth offers us an opportunity to view birth, life, and growth in a new and surprising way. Christmas can take on a new meaning if we enter into the mystery of the Christ Child developing and getting ready for birth in the last four weeks in the womb.

When we pay attention to the gestation of the Child, we see a powerful interplay of vulnerability, community, and dependence. Four weeks before his birth Jesus is most vulnerable: Mary and Joseph are his primary community, and he is dependent on Mary, his mother, for food and protection.

HOW TO USE THIS BOOK

The meditations in this book for each of the four weeks in Advent have a weekly theme and a daily reflection on the Child developing in the womb. Each day's meditation includes a simple mantra to recite, a theme, a Scripture reading and reflection on the reading, a description of the Child in the womb that is both developmentally accurate and imaginative, and a spiritual assignment.

Begin each day by saying the daily mantra, and repeat it as often as you can throughout the day. As you spend time with the Scripture passage, read it slowly. You may want to reread the passage, noting which word or phrase catches your attention. Ask yourself the following questions:

❋ What is happening in this passage?
❋ With whom or what do I identify in this passage?
❋ What is God saying to me in this passage?
❋ How can this passage help in my Advent preparation?

Following the Scripture passage and reflection is a description of what is happening to the Child in the womb. These meditations are based on our present-day understanding of the life of the fetus in the weeks before birth. This section attempts to keep the focus on the Christ Child, and offers us the opportunity to think about our own birth experiences.

At the end of every session you will have an opportunity to do a spiritual exercise—a simple guided meditation on the Scripture passage or the womb experience for that day. Feel free to adapt the meditation as you need to in order to aid your prayer. You may wish to repeat the exercise more than once, or return to it at the end of the day. The exercise is followed by simple questions and suggestions to take with you and ponder throughout the day.

✿

May this season of Advent be for you and your house
a time of new life.

The First Week of
Advent

GOD'S CREATION

Advent offers all of us a chance to be born again. We might well ask with Nicodemus, "How can anyone be born after having grown old? Can one enter a second time into the mother's womb and be born?" Jesus tells us that if we want to be part of the people of God we must be born "from above": "No one can enter the kingdom of God without being born of water and Spirit" (John 3:4–7). In truth, all of life is an ongoing opportunity for us to find new life and to get in touch with God's ongoing work of co-creating the world with us.

In the beginning God created everything. Created by God, we are called to be stewards of all that we have and receive from God. The mystery of the incarnation, Christmas, and Christ's coming invites us to enter fully into God's ongoing acts of creation and to participate joyfully in the reign of God.

Advent calls us to remember that God is our Creator. Remembering God's acts of creation, as well as God's acts of redemption, liberation, salvation, and grace, we grow in anticipation of the Child's coming at Christmas and on the last day. The first step in Advent is to remember that we are created by God and loved by God. The psalmist said it best:

Know that the LORD is God.
It is the LORD who made us,
    and we belong to God.

We are the people of God,
  sheep in God's pasture. (Psalm 100:3)

In this first week of Advent, we will pay attention to the creation story found in Genesis. We might just discover a new sense of hope for the world in these times, as we anticipate and participate in God's ongoing act of creation.

THIS WEEK IN THE WOMB

Thanks to all the maternal calcium, the Child has strong bones and a tough skull. His skull is firm but not rigid, and the plates are ready to give enough for the head to adjust in the birth process, when the time comes for the Child to work his way through the birth canal. This week, the fat is dimpling on his elbows, knees, wrists, and around his neck. The Child has a full face—baby cheeks that are guaranteed to catch the attention of children and adults alike. The cheeks are more noticeable because they have been filling out as he sucks his thumb in preparation for breastfeeding. His gums are very rigid and he has been practicing opening and closing his mouth and various sucking motions. He is ready to nurse.

It is a month before Mary is due. She is quite likely exhausted, worried, and more than a little curious. Joseph is probably experiencing a similar mixture of feelings. He is probably trying to grapple with his role in the whole series of events. On good days, he thanks God; on bad days, he wonders how he ever got into this. When they talk about all that has happened to them, they discover that they have many of the same joys, doubts, fears, and questions. When they pray, the awe-inspiring creation story in Genesis looms larger than ever before.

Advent 1: Sunday

O come, O come Emmanuel,
and give us your light today.

Advent is a time of remembering, appreciating, and antici-
pating the coming of the true Light into the world.

IN THE SCRIPTURES
Genesis 1:1–5

> In the beginning when God created the heavens and the
> earth, the earth was a formless void and darkness covered
> the face of the deep, while a wind from God swept over
> the face of the waters. Then God said, "Let there be light";
> and there was light. And God saw that the light was good;
> and God separated the light from the darkness. God called
> the light Day, and the darkness he called Night. And there
> was evening and there was morning, the first day.

God calls light into being and brings order out of chaos. We
see the power of the word of God, later manifested in the
Word. The creation story in Genesis offers powerful insights
about God. God does not fear the formless void, the darkness, and the chaos. We meet God as one who embraces and
enters into the chaos, bringing forth light. Our mothers can
tell us that pregnancy, though joyful at times, has many
moments of chaos, uncertainty, worry, emptiness, and a feeling of darkness.

When Advent is viewed alongside God's acts of creation,
we are reminded of the grounding of all human hope in God.
In the same way that life and light came out of the chaos and
the dark, wherever human hearts prepare for the birth of
Christ, faith assures all people of goodwill that light will come

from darkness, life will be born and possibilities will exist for a better life. Advent reminds us that God looks at the world and sees its goodness still. Wherever there is darkness and pain it is the will of God that humanity acts on the side of goodness and truth. God's act of creation continues to this day and Advent is a reminder that human beings are called into living deliberately to make the world a better place.

How do we remember, appreciate, and anticipate God's coming? The season invites the Christian community to remember that God created us and we belong to God. It is easy to forget that God the Creator is ultimately in charge of all things. In the bleak midwinter of the Advent season or as the ending of the year draws near with all its darkness and shadows, the reality of the God who enlightens our darkness by bringing light out of darkness is worth remembering.

IN THE WOMB

 The Child is surrounded by the darkness of the womb. Yet even in the darkness he is very sensitive to any light outside the womb.

As a child growing up in Jamaica, I was always afraid of the dark. There is something about the darkness that naturally frightens children, and even many adults. Back then in Jamaica, street lights were few and far between, so going outside at night or walking home late in the evening was not something I ever thought of doing.

My fear of the dark started to change around age four. I remember my father telling me, "Son, the darkness always gives way to the light." Although I was still afraid, I began to realize he was right: darkness always gives way to light. Only in my late teens did I lose my fear of the darkness. It took me many years to internalize the reality that the darkness in and of itself was not dangerous and could not hurt me.

I also remember my father telling me, "The darkest night is no match for a speck of light. Even inside of your mother's womb, where there is supposedly no light, there is light." I still do not know why father told me that. What was he thinking? I certainly did not know what to think at the time, and I was too scared to ask my father what he meant. When I next saw a pregnant woman, I told myself there is light in there—all is never dark.

In Brazil, they actually describe the birth of a child as the giving of light: *dar luz,* people say. It is their way of saying— and I delight in this—that a woman has brought a light into the world. When Advent comes, I always remember the creation story, and I especially think of the first day of creation when God dispels the darkness with light. I also think of the Child's birth as an act that also dispels the light. When we find ourselves in the dark or overwhelmed, what is our posture? Do we panic in the dark, or do we take measures to prepare ourselves for the light that must come? Let us turn toward the light with the Child.

SPIRITUAL EXERCISE

 Reread the passage from Genesis. Close your eyes and imagine the darkness of the womb. Try to imagine how the Child must look and feel at this stage of his development.

Think about the things that distract you and lead you away from the light. Slowly place your right hand over your heart and pray, "Lord, send your light into my life."

Now think of a person or a situation in need of light. Slowly extend your right hand, palm upward in blessing, and pray, "God, send your light wherever there is darkness."

For Today
 ❋ How might God be calling you to celebrate an Advent that is filled with light?
 ❋ Ask God to bring light to all of the dark places in your life today.
 ❋ Remember that Advent is about God bringing the light of Life into the darkness of the world.

Advent 1: Monday
O come, O come Emmanuel,
and let us think of heavenly things today.

Advent is a time to be attentive, careful, and deliberate.

IN THE SCRIPTURES
Genesis 1:6–8

> And God said, "Let there be a dome in the midst of the
> waters, and let it separate the waters from the waters." So
> God made the dome and separated the waters that were
> under the dome from the waters that were above the dome.
> And it was so. God called the dome Sky. And there was
> evening and there was morning, the second day.

On the second day of creation God sets the boundaries for further work. The sky and heavens are created as a buffer zone lim-
iting the role of chaos on the waters. Advent gives Christians an
opportunity to remember that creation takes time: God is not
finished with us or the world yet. The Genesis story shows that
the world was not built in a day. In addition, the writer of
Genesis shows an orderly series of creative acts that build on
each other. God is presented as attentive, deliberate, and careful. Working for life and love takes time.

Ignatius of Loyola, the founder of the Jesuits, after many
attempts at prayer realized that spiritual growth depended on
God's grace and the attentiveness of human beings to God's
presence, in and out of prayer. So Ignatius encouraged his
early companions to learn the art of attentiveness by paying
attention to all of life. Using the senses in and out of prayer
could bring a deeper awareness of God's activity in one's heart
and the world. By using awareness Jesuits deepened their rela-

tionship with God, whom they believed could be found and experienced in and through all things.

When we are aware, we are more creative. And when we are more aware of the things of God, God is more creative within us. It is not that our awareness causes God to be more active, but we become more conscious of the power of God in our lives.

Advent invites the Christian into a more careful and deliberate approach to God as a way of God-discovery and self-discovery. Careful attention in the spiritual life guarantees avoidance of certain common religious pitfalls. The Christian who pays attention stands in stark contrast to a present-day culture that emphasizes so much carelessness. Freedom and power frequently seduce the believer into accepting a lifestyle that is careless, irresponsible, and unrighteous. A mother handing a newborn to a family member captures the carefulness and attention required in the spiritual life. A father teaching a son to drive also illustrates the carefulness that forms part of the spiritual life. To be full of care takes us to a place where we notice how our thoughts, words, and actions have an impact on ourselves, those around us, and the world. All we have to do is look around and see: when we refuse to be careful or take care of ourselves, we end up ultimately doing serious damage.

Advent requires that we act deliberately and carefully; and with each passing day to recognize that there is an urgent need for Christians to love deliberately, forgive decidedly, and witness consciously to God's ongoing act of creation. The creation story and the Christmas story help us to see God as continuing the creative giving that beats at the heart of who God is and wants us to be.

IN THE WOMB

 By now, many of the Child's systems are mature. Blood circulation happens as it should and the senses are developing well. The Child has been opening and closing his mouth, probably already sucking his thumb. All this movement of the mouth is to prepare him for nursing; new forms of nourishment await the Child after his birth, forms that will provide nutrition and will further develop the facial muscles that will aid in his speech. Fed on the inside by his mother, the tricks of nursing and digestion will come later. Clearly, the womb is a temporary home. It will take almost two years for the digestive system to develop well.

I remember waiting for the birth of my son. Who knew that the whole pregnancy event could be so exciting, complicated, and fraught with so many emotions? Twenty weeks into the pregnancy, Kathy was told she needed a cervical cerclage (a simple operation to ensure that the baby didn't deliver early). Our son was in danger of being born before his time. After the operation, Kathy had to be on bedrest for the remaining months of the pregnancy. The only time she was allowed to leave the house was to see the doctors, which we did twice a month.

Waiting for a birth in situations like these is quite frightening. You never know what to expect. You hope for the best, but there is always a part of you that feels that disaster is just waiting to happen. Frightened as we were, we decided to love each other unconditionally, and grew very fond of our little child who was living on the edge.

So we prayed, supported each other, and waited. Every visit to the doctor was a new experience of the awesomeness of life. To see our son's heart beating and to hear the doctor looking at what was to us an indistinguishable mass and say, "He is perfect"—well, that felt like a creation experience. We could not help but enjoy the echo of God's own satisfied exclamation, "It is good."

SPIRITUAL EXERCISE

Reread the passage from Genesis. Close your eyes and imagine the darkness of the womb. Try to imagine how the Child must look and feel at this stage of his development.

Remember a time when you felt separated from God. What kept you separated and what brought you back to God? Make a note of the things that *separate* you from God. Then think about the things that make you feel *close to* God. Spend some time reflecting on the moments when you felt fearful and worried, and the times you knew God's love supporting you and giving you courage.

For Today
  ❊ How might God be calling you to celebrate Advent more boldly and deliberately?
  ❊ Ask God for the grace to love unconditionally despite your fears.
  ❊ Remember that Advent is about God's ongoing work of making all of creation whole again.

Advent 1: Tuesday

*O come, O come Emmanuel
and let us bear fruits that witness to your love today.*

Advent is a time to gather our spiritual resources and to bear fruits that witness to God's love.

IN THE SCRIPTURES
Genesis 1:9–13

And God said, "Let the waters under the sky be gathered together in one place, and let the dry land appear." And it was so. God called the dry land Earth, and the waters that were gathered together he called Seas. And God saw that it was good. Then God said, "Let the earth put forth vegetation: plants yielding seed, and fruit trees of every kind on earth that bear fruit with the seed in it." And it was so. The earth brought forth vegetation: plants yielding seed of

every kind, and trees of every kind bearing fruit with the
seed in it. And God saw that it was good. And there was
evening and there was morning, the third day.

On the third day, God gathers the water of chaos and con-
tains them so that the earth can be fruitful. Mother Earth is
born on this day and she immediately bursts into a life-giving
ministry. The call goes out to us: let human beings bring forth
fruit that will last. God continues creating without haste and
without waste, reminding us that love and creation take time.

The journey toward Christmas is a journey toward the
light, which demands a commitment to bear fruits worthy of
the followers of Christ. To be Christians, to be people of God,
requires a commitment to walk in the light: bearing fruits of
justice, love and compassion in deliberate ways. "You will
know them by their fruits," Jesus says (Matthew 7:16). His
words offer the Christian an invitation to understand that
part of the journey with Christ involves bearing fruit. The
Christian community, therefore, continues the work of creation by being fruitful and bringing forth into the world all
the love, humility, patience, and faith that come from an
experience of Love, an experience of Christ.

According to recent reports, millionaires will soon out-
number unemployed people in America. Many people are
bearing financial fruits and are doing quite well, while the
saying "the rich get richer and the poor poorer" is certainly as
true today as ever before. What is the Christian response in
light of the growing wealth and poverty? The challenge of
bringing good news still stands. And Christians who do well
financially face the extraordinary challenge of trying to figure
out how to share the fruits of their labor. The issue of wealth
stands at the center of Christian witness today.

Fruit trees in tropical countries show evidence of their
identity in their blossoming and bearing fruit. For example,
long before the blossoms come, there is a certain glow on the
leaves of the mango tree. Then the blossoms burst out in one
glorious day. On that day all doubts are removed: this is a

mango tree. From start to finish and in all stages of its life, a mango tree is a mango tree, but it arrives at its strongest identity at the point of bearing fruit. Fruit-bearing trees are never just celebrated for their fruit. At the moment of ripening, these trees have to endure a glorious assault: they must give up their fruit. And there is nothing more delightful than seeing young children climb up the branches of these fruit-laden trees to devour their gifts.

Fruit trees never resist giving up their fruit, and maybe this is one of the lessons from the third day of creation. Trees are created before human beings, and they have the capacity to remind us to be fruitful and not to cling to our possessions.

IN THE WOMB

The Child's body is preparing itself for life outside the womb. His fat percentage is about 15 percent, so that he will be warm after birth. This amazing fact of preparation for the next phase of life can give us some clues as to how to live the spiritual life. As we celebrate Advent, we have to ask ourselves how is it we are preparing ourselves to deal with the "cold" world in which we live. Fetal development is all about preparation for birth; in the same way, Advent is a call for all of us to get ready for new birth.

One of the earliest functions of a newborn is feeding, and if the cheeks are not developed properly feeding will be very difficult. The Child's cheeks have filled out in preparation for the milk he will need. How are our spiritual cheeks? Where do we find our spiritual nurture? We marvel at the human body in the womb and how it makes the appropriate response at the right time. We can learn from the Christ Child in the womb by asking ourselves where we need to "fatten" in order to make the most of the new experiences ahead of us.

SPIRITUAL EXERCISE

 Reread the passage from Genesis, using your senses to accompany God's creative actions. Hear the waters separating from the land. Smell the soil and vegetation, touch the ripe fruits and taste them, and see the vista of all things created before you.

Think about the things that you do for love or because of love. Then think of yourself as a tree. What kind of tree are you and what fruits do you produce? Repeat the phrase "Be fruitful and multiply" and see what significance these words have for you today.

Think of a situation where you may be called to bear more fruit. Slowly lift your hands to the heavens and say, "Lord, help me to bear fruit that will last." Hang there for a moment and feel the weight of what may be required of you.

For Today

※ How can this Advent be a more fruitful experience on your spiritual journey?

※ Ask God to show you how to make a difference in your home, school, or community.

※ Remember that Advent is about bearing fruits for God and witnessing to the reign of God.

Advent 1: Wednesday

O come, O come Emmanuel,
and let us be your light today.

Advent is a time to keep our eyes on the light, to draw near to the light, and to be the light.

IN THE SCRIPTURES
Genesis 1:14–19

> And God said, "Let there be lights in the dome of the sky to separate the day from the night; and let them be for signs and for seasons and for days and years, and let them be lights in the dome of the sky to give light upon the earth." And it was so. God made the two great lights—the greater light to rule the day and the lesser light to rule the night—and the stars. God sent them in the dome of the sky to give light upon the earth, to rule over the day and over the night, and to separate the light from the darkness. And God saw that it was good. And there was evening and there was morning, the fourth day.

On the fourth day of creation, order is brought to time: we have night and day, as a way of marking time and activities. Light, therefore, orders the darkness, apportioning the darkness to its rightful time and place. In the events of the fourth day, we are invited to examine the light and darkness that exist in every human heart.

For those experiencing the dark days of winter at this time, this passage is a call to remain hopeful that the sun will come out. Almost all the world religions hold celebrations with light as a central theme or event. As the days darken, the natural focus is on the importance of light in the ordering of our lives.

Christians believe that Jesus is the light of the world. It is the Christ Child who clarifies who God is and what it means to serve God. Advent provides a great opportunity to keep our eyes on the Child who is the light of the world and the light of God.

The Child did not merely talk about light, but let his light do the "walking." We are called to embody what it means to live in the light and be people of the light. Advent calls us to keep our eyes on the Child who is light because the world needs people who can witness to the light in their actions. Those who focus on the light naturally turn away from the darkness and expose it for what it is. It is easy for us to close in on ourselves and reject the light, but when we focus on the Child, we discover that there is no other way to live than to live in the light. When we accept that the Child is the light of the world, we accept our obligation to embody the light.

The Genesis story confirms that light and darkness are separated by God's design. One way of living in the light is to point out the areas in our world where darkness has taken control of the hearts and social situations of so many.

Closer to home, during Advent we have a wonderful opportunity to draw near the light. In our families, we can witness to the love of God by being more attentive to the needs of those closest to us. Tempted by the glitter of commercialism, we are called to find new ways of being the light of Christ. When we see acts of selfishness, we are called to respond with kindness. Where we see despair, we are called to bring hope. To paraphrase St. Francis, we could pray, "Lord, make me an instrument of your light."

IN THE WOMB

 The Child in the womb is sensitive to the light. When day dawns the Child turns toward the light and at night he turns toward wherever there is a lamp or brightness. Doctors call this turning toward the light an "orienting response." The Child seeks the light, even in the darkness of Mary's womb. I love to imagine his tiny upturned face like a blossom opening toward the sun.

As a young seminarian in Jamaica, I spent a lot of time as a Jesuit novice working in a home for the elderly. I recall noticing that the oldest people in the home always sat where they could turn toward the light. They did not sit directly in the sun or in the light, but they sat in such a way that they could feel the light or move toward a light. I remember asking one of the women why she did this. "It makes me feel like a baby, like a child in the womb," she told me.

Light draws the Child for two reasons: light entices everything it touches, and light beckons him to the world outside the womb. On the first day of creation God called forth light into existence, setting in place the reality that all living things would forever depend on light. Our light is the Child, "the true light, which enlightens everyone" (John 1:9).

SPIRITUAL EXERCISE

 Reread the passage from Genesis. Close your eyes and imagine the darkness of the womb. Try to imagine how the Child must look and feel at this stage of his development.

Visualize yourself in the womb of your mother. See yourself turning toward the light. Place a candle before you and just gaze at it, or picture a light and see yourself walking toward it. Think of a situation where you can bring light. Slowly place your hands over your eyes and say, "Lord, let me see the light" or "Lord, let me be the light."

For Today

❋ How can this Advent be a time of turning toward the light?

❋ Ask God to show you how to walk in the light.

❋ Remember that Advent is about bringing light to those in need and speaking words of love.

Advent 1: Thursday

O come, O come Emmanuel,
and let us be your living presence today.

Advent is a time of remembering that God is abundant life and that we are called to share our abundance with others.

IN THE SCRIPTURES
Genesis 1:20–23

> And God said, "Let the waters bring forth swarms of living creatures, and let birds fly above the earth across the dome of the sky." So God created the great sea monsters and every living creature that moves, of every kind, with which the waters swarm, and every winged bird of every kind. And God saw that it was good. God blessed them, saying, "Be fruitful and multiply and fill the waters in the seas, and let birds multiply on the earth." And there was evening and there was morning, the fifth day.

Throughout the Genesis story, the theme is one of bearing fruit, producing beauty, and producing life. As the story of creation continues, we see that every aspect of creation is invited into the life-producing agenda. What a powerful reminder to all of us that we are capable of great acts of creativity—you in your small corner and I in mine.

Some years ago, a question floated around social gatherings: Would you rather be ignored or hated? The underlying premise of this question was that those who are ignored are unproductive, have little impact or value. This Advent we can open our eyes to a new reality, one that paves the way to life lived more deeply, to eternal life. To see the Child is to see him in our fellow human beings, it is to see him in the stranger, the poor, the marginalized, the other, even the enemy.

We are to go out and see the Child in those who are perceived as unproductive or worthless. Over and over again throughout our Scriptures, we meet God affirming life. Theologians from Latin America describe the poor on their continent as people dying before their time. They die before their time because even the basics of life are denied them by the greed of many who have more than their fair share of the world's resources. How will the poor be able to feed and educate their children? How will they provide their children adequate health care? Where is life for these poor who are dying before their time? What about the poor in our own country, in Africa, in the Middle East? What does "producing" mean for these people who quite frequently do not even have the bare necessities of life?

A journalist once wrote that the food thrown out from restaurants in the United States could feed the poor several times over in many developing countries. Advent challenges us to think on these things, to think on the project of life, to think about the ignored and hated.

The inequality in today's world that leads to death gets more frightening when we realize how even something as simple and essential as water gets exploited. Once again it is the poor who have to walk miles to get clean water. So many of the poor and their children die before their time because they are forced to drink polluted water.

We often spend our life searching for signs of God's love, when all around us the creation speaks loudly of God's ongoing care for us. The birds of the air and the fish of the sea remind us of God's desire that all of humanity have life in abundance. When we accept that God is a God of life, we are free to trust completely in who God is.

One of the most poignant teachings of Jesus is this: "Look at the birds of the air; they neither sow nor reap nor gather into barns, and yet your heavenly Father feeds them. Are you not of more value than they?" (Matthew 6:26). God's desire for the animals of the water and the air is the same for us: we are called to be fruitful and multiply.

We are called to live in such a way that we help each other grow into our best selves. Advent is a powerful reminder for us to remember the poor, because the Child we celebrate is one who was poor, and one who dedicated his ministry in service of the poor.

IN THE WOMB

The Child's bones are developing and continue to grow in a way that provides shape to his tiny body. Bones have to be firm and strong, but in the womb the developing fetus needs a more flexible bone structure. The act of birth is probably the only time human beings will flex, twist, and contort their body in such a unique way.

One lesson we can learn from the development of the Child's bones is the need to be firm, but not too firm. Our greatest temptation as human beings is to be rigid. Celebrating Advent calls us to pay attention to the life of Jesus and how he practiced a ministry of flexibility. Remember the many people he healed even when he felt tired, or the marginalized people with whom he ate and drank despite the criticism of the religious authorities. Being a Christian today requires that we develop strong bones that can stand firm against oppression and evil, and malleable bones capable of understanding and compassion, bones that are strong and flexible enough to adapt to changing circumstances.

Some years ago I heard a Buddhist story that went like this. A teacher asked, "What do you have in your hands?" "Nothing," said the student. "Then let it go," responded the teacher. I am still not sure I understand fully what this story means. I believe that it has to do with learning to let go, learning to be flexible, and learning not to live a life of grasping.

SPIRITUAL EXERCISE

Reread the passage from Genesis. Close your eyes and imagine the darkness of the womb. Try to imagine how the Child must look and feel at this stage of his development. See him developing slowly, but surely. Visualize the bones of his body, how they continue to harden and will continue hardening after birth. Focus on the vertebrae and how they connect to each other. Try to sense how fragile the Child is at this time.

Think of a person or a situation with whom or in which you were too rigid or stubborn. Ask for light and understanding. Place your right hand on your head and say slowly, "Loving God, give me the mind of Christ."

Slowly rise and stretch the full length of your body, or remain seated and run your hands firmly over your limbs. Then say, "Lord, give me the grace to be flexible."

For Today

   ❊ How can this Advent be a more flexible experience on your spiritual journey?
   ❊ Ask God to show you how to be firm and yet not rigid, strong and yet gentle.
   ❊ Remember that Advent is about standing firm on the promises of God, but living gracefully in the gentle hope of Christ's coming.

Advent 1: Friday

O come, O come Emmanuel,
and let us be your people today.

Advent is a time to remember that we are created in the image of God, and we share with all creation in God's life.

IN THE SCRIPTURES
Genesis 1:27–31

So God created humankind in his image,
  in the image of God he created them;
    male and female he created them.
God blessed them, and God said to them, "Be fruitful and multiply, and fill the earth and subdue it; and have dominion over the fish of the sea and over the birds of the air and over every living thing that moves upon the earth." God said, "See, I have given you every plant yielding seed that is upon the face of all the earth, and every tree with seed in its fruit; you shall have them for food. And to every beast of the earth, and to every bird of the air, and to everything that creeps on the earth, everything that has the breath of life, I have given every green plant for food." And it was so. God saw everything that he had made, and indeed, it was very good. And there was evening and there was morning, the sixth day.

In this version of the creation story, God makes "humankind, male and female, in the image of God." What a refreshing call to see each person as loved, valued, and honored by God. How would human history have been different if we had accepted this reality of the creation story? What will it take for us to accept each other—male, female, black, white, Jew,

Muslim, and Christian, all manner of persons and groups—as valued members of God's family?

God reaches the final day of creation. Everything is in order and ready for human beings to take their place in the created order. Even though human beings have a unique place and role, we get the sense from this narrative that all of creation exists in an unbreakable chain. We will forever stand before God as individuals forming part of a community. We are always a gift to each other. In God's plan, we see the interdependence and connection of all things. Human life takes on a whole different perspective when lived in the realization that we owe our life and all that we have to God. The knowledge that we owe our very existence to God can serve to orient all our actions.

Native Americans and many other indigenous cultures put great emphasis on the spiritual nature of all created things. Allegedly "advanced" cultures have moved away from believing that objects have spirits and a life of their own. Yet when we examine the story of creation, we see that as human beings we are brothers and sisters of the birds and the fish, the dogs and whales and elephants, the sun and the moon. We all share the same beginning, the same genes, and the same end.

Everything comes from God. Part of our spiritual journey is to do the detective work required to find the fingerprints of God on everything and in every human being around us. We sometimes forget that every human being is a creature of God. The poor, the drunk, the addict, and the stranger have God's fingerprints all over them; they have our genes, because we are all brothers and sisters. To ignore the other is to ignore God. When Jesus calls us to true service and love by reminding us that whatever we do to the least we do to God, he is reminding us to find God in all things. Our journey to see the babe in Bethlehem takes on added significance if we recognize that the Child to be born is a victim of exclusion.

So much of Advent is about waiting. When we wait on God, we draw near to God and when God waits on us, God draws near to us. Part of drawing near to God is discovering God in each other, and finding God in those who suffer, those who search for God, and those who need God.

IN THE WOMB

The Child gets fatter and fatter with each passing moment. His toenails and fingernails are grown. He is beyond the danger zone—which means he could be born today and still be all right. Mary's womb is quite active as it contracts frequently and causes her back pains. With each contraction of the womb, the Child receives more blood that brings necessary nutrients. He must also be detecting the changes in his surroundings and experiencing the discomfort of less space to move around.

One interesting aspect of waiting at this time is the abundance of contractions. Today we call them Braxton-Hicks contractions, or false labor pains. We need to remember that not every pain is labor. How can we stay grounded as the events in our world resemble what some call the end times? How can we remain focused and centered in the midst of our own uncertainties? How can we remain calm amid the contractions of our lives?

SPIRITUAL EXERCISE

Reread the passage from Genesis. Close your eyes and imagine the darkness of the womb. Try to imagine how the Child must look and feel at this stage of his development.

Imagine your mother and the pain she must have felt before your birth. What do you feel toward your mother? Then imagine yourself within the womb, two or three weeks away from birth. What are you sensing? What state are you in as you get ready for birth?

Think of the Child and Mary. Slowly place your hand on your stomach and say, "Lord, let me give birth to light" or "Lord, let me not be afraid of the suffering that comes before

new birth." Spend some time thanking God that you are
wonderfully made.

For Today

❊ How can this Advent be more life-giving?

❊ Ask God to deepen your faith during painful or difficult moments.

❊ Remember that before life happens, chaos, pain, and confusion may reign, but they will not last forever.

Advent 1: Saturday

O come, O come Emmanuel,
and teach us to rest in your presence today.

Advent is a time to rest in the Lord.

IN THE SCRIPTURES
Genesis 2:1–3

Thus the heavens and the earth were finished, and all their
multitude. And on the seventh day God finished the work
that he had done, and he rested on the seventh day from
all the work that he had done. So God blessed the seventh
day and hallowed it, because on it God rested from all the
work that he had done in creation.

God has created all that is needed, fulfilling his words and
intentions. At the end of every action God has expressed
pleasure, pride, and love. The narrative tells us that God saw
that it was good. After everything is created, one thing
remains; it is just as important as all that has preceded. God
chooses to end the work and rest. God rests. It is doing nothing, but doing something that is just as important as everything else. God by resting creates the Sabbath.

A Jewish friend of mine once said, "The best praise we can give to God is to imitate God by resting, especially on the Sabbath." Despite all the technological advances billed to make our lives easier, we are even more distracted and exhausted. What a difference it would make if we built in moments of rest and meditation every day of our lives.

As the celebration of Christmas has become more commercialized, the days of Advent have become increasingly hectic. In a strange way, our preparations for Christmas distract us, making it hard for these weeks to be a time of restful preparation. Few people find the time to be quiet, reflecting on the "reason for the season." Could it be that we enjoy the busyness of the time because it prevents us from looking at the reality of what the season is all about? Are we busying ourselves in order not to pay attention to all that birth entails—our birth and that of the Child?

The Child offers us rest, because we are so in need of it. We forget the importance of physical rest and we forget the importance of spiritual rest. We work harder and harder, working longer and longer hours. Our economic system scares us into ever-increasing productivity. Production drives us beyond our human limits and cares not whether we die from overwork or fatigue. Work, family, and church leave us exhausted. We need rest.

Some of us take better care of our physical health. We do not let the television rob us of our needed sleep, nor do we let meetings, parties, or friends eat away at the time we should spend relaxing with family or just resting. It seems that to find time to relax requires a determined effort. There is a discipline and aggressiveness in claiming the space to rest, relax, and be free. Physical rest is an important and essential spiritual principle, especially when we use the time to ponder the mysteries of God and to worship.

Remembering the need for physical rest and holidays can remind us of the need for spiritual rest and holy days. Advent presents us with almost four weeks to focus on the birth of the Child. Liturgically, it is not a rushed time; there is time for silence. In the quiet, we look inward to focus on God's presence among us, on the Child who is coming. We also look around us and notice the hope and despair in our world. We search for clues leading us to the places and ways where we can bring God's rest.

Advent offers us the opportunity to rest on holy ground, to see every moment as holy and to know that wherever we are is holy ground. "Remember the sabbath day, and keep it holy. Six days you shall labor and do all your work. But the seventh day is a sabbath to the LORD your God; you shall not do any work" (Exodus 20:8–10).

IN THE WOMB

As the birth of the Child draws nearer, things get more and more uncomfortable for Mary. She longs for a rest from all her labors. She can probably feel the Child's legs, arms, or bottom if she caresses her stomach in a certain way. She can feel the Child moving, and his movements may cause her pain or laughter. In the womb, the Child receives more and more nutrients and antibodies to prepare him for life outside the womb. Being so close to birth, the Child is at rest.

Even God needed a rest after creating human beings. At times Mary is exhausted and ready to deliver her heavy load; at other times she feels energized by her excitement. There is a simple lesson for all of us in this: Hold on. Giving birth to new life of any kind is never an easy experience. Sometimes more effort is required of us as the "delivery" approaches, and we are called to rest when we need to—but we rest in the Lord.

SPIRITUAL EXERCISE

Reread the passage from Genesis. Close your eyes and imagine the darkness of the womb. Try to imagine how the Child must look and feel at this stage of his development. Imagine the blood flowing from the placenta; look at his face, his hands, his fingers and toes. Imagine the Child at rest in the womb. What does he look like? What are you sensing and feeling? Slowly place your hand on your stomach and say, "Lord, still my soul within me."

For Today

    ❋ How can this Advent be a time of sabbath rest for you?

    ❋ What does it mean for you to rest in the Lord? Ask God to show you how to rest spiritually.

    ❋ Remember that prayer and spiritual reading bring light and rest to our souls.

The Second Week of
Advent

GOD ANNOUNCES
LIFE AND BIRTH

The Bible begins with the creation story and everything that follows reveals human beings interacting with God. The Scriptures reveal God responding to our search for God by seeking to grace humanity with abundant life. It is in the experience of birth and new life that human beings experience one aspect of God's caring love.

Repeatedly in the Scriptures, we meet God answering the prayer of barren women and see human beings responding to God's benevolence in the way they name their children. God does not form human beings out of dust and then abandon them, but comes to them repeatedly, especially in the experience of birth. Time and time again, God sends angels to announce the birth of a child. Maybe one often overlooked truth in these stories is that God pays attention to the birth of every human being—angels not only accompany adults, but are present in the whole experience of life. God is part of every moment of our lives.

The season of Advent stands as one of the most poignant reminders that God is the source and creator of all good things, especially the gift of life. During this second week of Advent, we will pay attention to some of these birth stories, perhaps discovering something new about God, the characters in the Bible, ourselves, and our families.

THIS WEEK IN THE WOMB

The Child is now practicing breathing movements. His lungs are almost developed and he is prepared for life outside the womb. His grasp is firm, and he probably has been clutching the umbilical cord. He is now more sensitive to and aware of the things happening in his mother's body and outside her. He turns more often toward the light this week. The Child has not stopped growing yet, developing fat at the rate of a half-ounce each day. He has probably dropped down into Mary's pelvis, moving slowly toward the birth canal. There is a lot of pressure on her ribs and internal organs. The Child's intestines are accumulating meconium, the waste products from the liver, pancreas, and gall bladder.

Advent 2: Sunday

Emmanuel, show your glory within me,
and give me your Holy Spirit today.

Advent is a time to remember the wonderful works of God, the *yes* of Mary, and the mystery of the incarnation.

IN THE SCRIPTURES
Luke 1:26–38

In the sixth month the angel Gabriel was sent by God to a town in Galilee called Nazareth, to a virgin engaged to a man whose name was Joseph, of the house of David. The virgin's name was Mary. And he came to her and said, "Greetings, favored one! The Lord is with you." But she was perplexed by his words and pondered what sort of greeting this might be. The angel said to her, "Do not be afraid, Mary, for you have found favor with God. And now, you will conceive in your womb and bear a son, and you will name him Jesus. He will be great, and will be called the Son of the Most High, and the Lord God will give to him the throne of his ancestor David. He will reign over the house of Jacob forever, and of his kingdom there will be no end." Mary said to the angel, "How can this be, since I am a virgin?" The angel said to her, "The Holy Spirit will come upon you, and the power of the Most High will overshadow you; therefore the child to be born will be holy; he will be called Son of God. And now, your relative Elizabeth in her old age has also conceived a son; and this is the sixth month for her who was said to be barren. For nothing will be impossible with God." Then Mary said, "Here am I, the servant of the Lord; let it be with me according to your word." Then the angel departed from her.

Luke's story of the Annunciation centers on God's desire to experience life as a human being and the power of a young woman's brave *yes* to God. Looking at Mary and looking at God, we see an invitation for us to examine how God is born in us, and we in God. Theologian Dietrich Bonhoeffer said that the most important ingredient for good community is an ability to listen to the other. This encounter between Mary and the angel is a tender moment that shows us the power of listening.

The angel Gabriel was sent by God to a town named Nazareth. Politically, culturally, and historically, Nazareth has no claim to fame. Add to this insignificant town an insignificant virgin girl called Mary. She is chosen by God because she has found favor with God. Once again, there is no way to explain the choice of God. God's activities often read like fairy tales. Whether we hold to a belief in the virgin birth or not, there is something powerful in the fact that this young woman—poor and insignificant—is to become the mother of the Savior. For the poor throughout the world, for teenage mothers, for those who are ignored by the powerful, Mary holds up proof that God chooses the poor and the simple to work wonders.

Saying *yes* to God daily is the most countercultural and productive thing we can do in and with our lives. When we look at Mary's life, we see a young girl brave enough to accept God's word even though it would cause her immeasurable suffering, confusion, and pain. What a far cry from the way we live our lives: we want our will to be done and done all the time. What would it be like to give God's will a chance in our lives?

The Holy Spirit overshadowed Mary as a means of giving birth to the Child, and we are called to be filled with the Holy Spirit as a means of giving birth to Jesus in the world. The Child embodies concretely the project and will of God: in Jesus, God has entered human history forever.

Quite likely Mary had no idea what the angel meant. In the same way, we are still not sure what exactly God's project for the world is, but Mary says *yes* in faith. Sometimes we hesitate to say *yes* in faith because we think that God must not be interested in us. God wants something special for each of us, and we can only discover what it is by saying *yes* and trusting God. There is something waiting to be born in all of us. Advent is a time to say *yes* to that new life.

We learn a great message about God in this passage: the wonderful works of God issue from a God who is gratuitously generous. Where would we choose to be born? Where would we choose our child to be born? Where would God announce the birth of Jesus today?

IN THE WOMB

 Two weeks before delivery the lungs are almost developed, almost ready for life outside the womb. Inside the womb, the Child is ready, yet patient.

I recall going to birth classes with my wife. Breathing was the best way to prepare for birth, one nurse's aide said.

Breathing consciously and deliberately is one way to live the spiritual life.

As we prepare for Christmas we can learn a lesson from the Child by breathing where we are. The Child gets ready to be born by doing what is necessary on the inside, in his mother's womb.

There is a popular saying, "Breathe easy." For Mary, it is still not a time to relax, but for the Child within her, there is regular breathing within the amniotic fluid. Because the Child will soon have to breathe air for himself, his lungs are developing in such a way to prepare him for that.

Advent is our womb experience, preparing us to burst onto our individual stages and live and breathe in the Spirit of God.

SPIRITUAL EXERCISE

Reread the passage from Luke. Close your eyes and imagine the darkness of the womb. Try to imagine how the Child must look and feel at this stage of his development. Imagine him breathing within the womb. The umbilical cord provides him with all the nutrients and oxygen he needs. Visualize his connection to Mary his mother.

Now imagine yourself connected to God. What comes to mind? What do you need to receive from God to breathe spiritually? Notice your breathing and imagine that you are breathing out the things that are not of God and breathing in the things that are of God. Say, "Breathe in me, breath of God."

For Today
* ❋ How can this Advent be a breath of fresh air?
* ❋ Ask for the grace to be more aware of the Holy Spirit in your life.
* ❋ Remember that we are called to be the incarnate presence of God in the world.

Advent 2: Monday

Emmanuel, show your glory within me,
and help me to see your face today.

Advent is a time to remember God cares for all people, and comes to find the outcast and the lonely.

IN THE SCRIPTURES
Genesis 16:7–11

The angel of the LORD found her by a spring of water in the wilderness, the spring on the way to Shur. And he said, "Hagar, slave-girl of Sarai, where have you come from and where are you going?" She said, "I am running away from my mistress Sarai." The angel of the LORD said to her, "Return to your mistress, and submit to her." The angel of the LORD also said to her, "I will so greatly multiply your offspring that they cannot be counted for the multitude." And the angel of the LORD said to her,

"Now you have conceived and shall bear a son;
you shall call him Ishmael,
   for the LORD has given heed to your affliction."

This passage presents a most intriguing incident in the life Abraham, the father of faith, or you could say, the family of faith. On the run from barren and angry Sarah, haughty and boastful Hagar encounters the loneliness of a life on the run. Hagar prefigures for all peoples God's care for the outcast and reinforces our belief that God listens to prayer. God comes to her and names her child. In a powerful way, she prefigures Mary of Nazareth even more than Sarah does.

God hears Hagar's cry and comes to her. God tells her about her life. God promises to bless her. We read that it is

Abraham who named the child, but we must not forget that God first tells Hagar the name of the child. Our mothers connect us to God in so many ways.

To think about the human story or history is also to think about our story and history. Amid Hagar's personal tragedies, she experiences God coming to meet her in the moment when things seem most desperate. Her son becomes the father of a great nation and fulfills the promises God made to her. Her story encourages us to know that we are never abandoned. Where is God in our story? When have we been on the run? How does God meet us on the run? How do we experience God's love? How is God promising to bless the things we create?

Throughout the Bible, we see time and time again how women witness to the power of God. Today, we know the witness that many women have given to our country and to our faith communities. Hagar must have taught Abraham something about love. She must have taught him about yearning for God, for others, and for goodness. In Matthew's genealogy, Jesus is linked to Abraham. There is no way to think of Jesus and Abraham without remembering Hagar. The Child is related to her through Abraham, and it is no small wonder that much of his ministry was done on behalf of people with stories similar to Hagar's.

IN THE WOMB

 The womb is extended and heavy, and Mary is feeling much discomfort at this time. She could not have predicted all that she would feel and experience during these last weeks. In this sense, she is a little like Hagar: surprised by God and life.

My wife and I were told we might lose our child because he was making his way out of the womb too early. Ironically, after my wife had endured months of bedrest, the due date came and went, and our son seemed content to stay in the womb for a lot longer than the doctors could have predicted.

We tend to glamorize pregnancy and childbirth by planning and buying everything to assure our own comfort. We give less thought to life in the womb, but here is an important fact to keep in mind: inside the child's intestines, a dark-green mass of waste product accumulates. The child is dwelling next to its own waste material and there is no way out, for now. What a lesson about accepting the things we cannot change.

We all have unpleasant memories that accompany us on our journey of life. When faced with unpleasant memories or experiences, our first impulse can be a desire to flee, like Hagar. What would it be like for us to sit and live with all the waste products of our lives—the moments of shame, pain, conflict, self-hate, envy, and temptations? Yet the Child does not want to be born before his time. How about us?

SPIRITUAL EXERCISE

Reread the passage from Genesis. Close your eyes and imagine the darkness of the womb. Try to imagine how the Child must look and feel at this stage of his development. Imagine his umbilical cord, and look at him as he is connected to it. What does the connection look like? The umbilical cord provides him with all the nutrients and oxygen he needs. Visualize his ability to hold on to it, but also to let it go.

Now imagine yourself holding on to the things you hold dear and letting them go. Say, "Lord, I consider all as rubbish, and glory only in knowing you."

For Today
   ❉ How can this Advent be a time of letting go?
   ❉ Ask for the grace to hold on to what matters
      spiritually.
   ❉ Remember that we are called to be faithful even when
      we feel abandoned by family, friends, and God.

Advent 2: Tuesday

Emmanuel, show your glory within me,
and bring me the gift of laughter today.

Advent is time to be open to divine intervention, a time to laugh, and a time to give birth.

IN THE SCRIPTURES
Genesis 18:9–14

> They said to him, "Where is your wife Sarah?" And he said, "There, in the tent." Then one said, "I will surely return to you in due season, and your wife Sarah shall have a son." And Sarah was listening at the tent entrance behind him. Now Abraham and Sarah were old, advanced in age; it had ceased to be with Sarah after the manner of women. So Sarah laughed to herself, saying, "After I have grown old, and my husband is old, shall I have pleasure?" The LORD said to Abraham, "Why did Sarah laugh, and say, 'Shall I indeed bear a child, now that I am old?' Is anything too wonderful for the LORD? At the set time I will return to you, in due season, and Sarah shall have a son."

Three angels pay Abraham a visit. At first Abraham does not recognize them as angels, but when they predict that Sarah will have a child, Abraham realizes they are heavenly beings. Their message evokes laughter of incredulity in Sarah, which she later denies. Uncertain and incredulous laughter later gives way to rejoicing.

Sarah had given up on ever having a child. She must have held on to a lot of resentment, shame, and self-pity, because she lived in a culture that valued childbearing as the supreme blessing from God. Who knows how Abraham treated her because of her barrenness? Who knows how she treated herself? Yet Sarah had a long life, an empty womb, and a heart filled with laughter. Some of us break out in tears when the sensitive aspects of our lives are named. Some of us break down when people name the thing or things we lack. Sarah laughed. She laughed because she found the whole thing funny. She laughed because it was a little embarrassing to even think of her, so advanced in age, pregnant.

Laugh, Sarah, laugh, because nothing is too wonderful for God. Laugh in the face of God, because that is what all your emotions lead you to do. Laugh and let it out. Laugh and make room for new life. Would to God we could laugh at ourselves a lot more. Oh the joy and blessings that would enter the tight spaces of our life if we could laugh at how unbelievable good tidings can be sometimes. How blessed we would be if we could laugh at how ridiculous we are most of the time.

IN THE WOMB

 The Child is now more sensitive to and aware of the things happening in his mother's body and outside her. The Child hears muffled sounds outside the womb, and turns increasingly toward voices and other sounds he recognizes. He is constantly practicing opening and closing his mouth. What could we learn from this? When we have no words to speak, how do we train ourselves for the moment when we will need to speak?

Sarah must have felt at one and the same time like a mother and a child. At her age, she must have been saying to herself, "Admit it, as much fun as this is, it is ridiculous." She must have learned a lot from sitting there with her own diminished energy, waiting and waiting, sensing the life within her. She must have known that her life was waning, even as a new life was growing within her. Yet imagine how Sarah and Abraham must have welcomed and cherished their son—his very presence constantly reminded them that God intervenes on behalf of those who trust God even in tight spaces.

SPIRITUAL EXERCISE

Reread the passage from Genesis. Close your eyes and imagine the darkness of the womb. Try to imagine how the Child must look and feel at this stage of his development. Look at him as he turns toward Mary's voice, her cries, her laughter, her songs. Watch him react to every movement Mary makes. In the womb he is already moving his limbs, even in very cramped surroundings.

Now visualize yourself turning toward the voices who have brought comfort or laughter in your life. What would Jesus' voice sound like? Say, "I want to turn toward you, the Child."

For Today
- ✴ How can this Advent be a time of turning toward the voice of God?
- ✴ Ask for the grace to speak words of comfort and strength to others.
- ✴ Remember that we are called to believe in the love, light, miracles, and wonders of God.

Advent 2: Wednesday

Emmanuel, show your glory within me, and love the places where I feel unloved today.

Advent is a time to be seen, heard, remembered, and blessed by God.

IN THE SCRIPTURES
Genesis 29:31–32; 30:1–2, 22–24

When the LORD saw that Leah was unloved, he opened her womb; but Rachel was barren. Leah conceived and bore a son, and she named him Reuben; for she said, "Because the LORD has looked upon my affliction, surely now my

husband will love me.". . . When Rachel saw that she bore
Jacob no children, she envied her sister; and she said to
Jacob, "Give me children, or I shall die!" Jacob became
very angry with Rachel and said, "Am I in the place of
God, who has withheld from you the fruit of the
womb?". . . Then God remembered Rachel, and God heeded her and opened her womb. She conceived and bore a
son, and said, "God has taken away my reproach"; and she
named him Joseph, saying, "May the LORD add to me
another son!"

God feels the pain of Leah, Jacob, and Rachel and grants
them their wish to have offspring. When God "saw that Leah
was unloved, he opened her womb"—Scripture does not get
any more powerful than this. But the story continues, "then
God remembered Rachel, and God heeded her and opened
her womb"—Scripture does not get any more tender than
this. God creates new life for Leah, Jacob and Rachel by blessing them with children.

Do we feel seen, heard, remembered, and blessed by God?
In our busy lives, we easily forget that we are precious in the
sight of God. "If God so clothes the grass of the field, which
is alive today and tomorrow is thrown into the oven, will he
not much more clothe you—you of little faith?" (Matthew
6:30). Indeed, it is our faith in God that reminds us we are
forever in the sight of God. Our search for meaning as
Christians is to come to this realization of knowing that we
are always in God's view. To live in the sight of God calls us
to trust the providence and the workings of God.

The more we attune our lives to this reality, the more we
take on the eyes of God. Numerous times throughout the
Scriptures we hear God described as seeing the suffering of
individuals and entire peoples. God does see the suffering of
our hearts, which we try so hard to conceal from one another. God sees the suffering of millions of poor and homeless
people, whom our society tries to hide from our view. God
sees us when we are Leah, needing to give birth. God sees us

when we are Jacob, struggling to make sense of God's promises. God sees us when we are Rachel, desperate to have things work out.

Advent is also a time to be heard by God. To approach Christmas without prayer is to go to the airport without a ticket. God wants to hear our prayers, our hopes, our conflict, our pain, and our joys. In an ever more talkative society, we have distanced ourselves from talking to our Creator. As Christmas approaches, we spend a lot of time talking to friends, but few of us spend sufficient time giving God a chance to hear us. God knows that we are happy, but God wants us to sing thanks. God knows that we hurt, but God wants us to proclaim a ballad. God knows that we can speak, but God wants to hear our voices. How often do we cry out to God? How often do we sing God's praises? When was the last time we said "I love you" to God?

IN THE WOMB

With birth approaching, the Child continues to grow, developing fat at the rate of a half-ounce a day. It is a slower growth than the earlier gestation stages, but still there is growth. The power of the Child in the womb is that he keeps growing, and so life outside the womb is really a continuation of life in the womb. Leah, Jacob, and Rachel are a continuation of a story started with Adam and Eve, and my wife and I are a continuation of that same story.

After an ectopic pregnancy and a miscarriage, my wife and I could not decide whether we felt like Leah or Rachel. We did feel unloved and we did feel forgotten, and our emotions were not pretty. During that time I forgot how to pray—prayer really seemed useless then. I remember sharing this with my spiritual director, a wise priest who encouraged me to look at my wife, remember my wife, and hold my wife. "Do not stop praying," he told me. Ultimately, he encouraged us to be for each other the life we wanted to bear. Within weeks, we were pregnant.

Do we remember that we are beginning again, starting over and growing? It is a joyful season and also a difficult one. By the end of the year, the last thing most of us want is to be asked to improve and to grow. The weather and the light contribute to a desire to give up, to lie down and not do much. For us as Christians the call goes out to wake up and be watchful. Pay attention, the Scriptures remind us over and over again. In the quiet and in the cold, we listen attentively to God, and we warm our hearts by drawing close to God. Who knows the birth places deep within us that God will open?

How do we grow in the areas where we feel forgotten by God? How do we grow when we feel barren like Leah and Rachel? How do we grow in the quiet and the dark? Spend some time today reflecting on your spiritual journey in the dark night of the soul. Let us be still, let us be contemplative in our actions, not for our own sake, but because God needs us to be light, even as the night approaches.

SPIRITUAL EXERCISE

Reread the passage from Genesis. Close your eyes and imagine the darkness of the womb. Try to imagine how the Child must look and feel at this stage of his development. Think of Mary and what she must be feeling at this time. Say, "Lord, keep me on the path toward you."

For Today

  ❋ How can this Advent be a time of knowing yourself loved?
  ❋ Ask God for the strength to grow where you need to grow, even in the barren places.
  ❋ Remember that God keeps watch over us.

Advent 2: Thursday

Emmanuel, show your glory within me,
and restore and nourish me today.

Advent is a time to remember that all of humanity is connected and we are called to celebrate the ways God blesses others.

IN THE SCRIPTURES
Ruth 4:13–17

> So Boaz took Ruth and she became his wife. When they came together, the LORD made her conceive, and she bore a son. Then the women said to Naomi, "Blessed be the LORD, who has not left you this day without next-of-kin; and may his name be renowned in Israel! He shall be to you a restorer of life and a nourisher of your old age; for your daughter-in-law who loves you, who is more to you than seven sons, has borne him." Then Naomi took the child and laid him in her bosom, and became his nurse. The women of the neighborhood gave him a name, saying, "A son has been born to Naomi." They named him Obed; he became the father of Jesse, the father of David.

God moves in mysterious and wonderful ways, bringing the unexpected to Boaz, Ruth and Naomi. God emphasizes that family goes beyond blood ties, as Naomi accepts the child of Ruth as her own son. The whole book of Ruth is worth reading for its powerful message of life and love.

In the gospels, over and over again, Jesus informed his disciples and the crowds that being part of God's family does not depend primarily on family ties. "For whoever does the will of my Father in heaven is my brother and sister and mother"

(Matthew 12:50). We are all connected in the reign of God; through God's love we are all brothers and sisters.

This is good news and bad news, because there is nothing more difficult than seeing *those people* as related to us. To love conservatives, liberals, Democrats, Republicans, Muslims, Jews, agnostics, atheists, thieves, rapists, bigots, racists, the poor, the unemployed, the rich CEO, and the sick demands more than most of us can handle.

From a distance, we can profess our love for these groups, these people, but at a neighborly proximity, we all break down. We are called to love the strangers and to be a neighbor to them. To make the journey to the manger and while passing the wounded, the sick, and the poor—the other—along the roadside does us no good. To make the journey to the manger and miss the baby dying along the roadside is useless. Many of us forget that the Child has already been born: when we journey to the manger, we are taking the Child with us. We bring to the manger who we are and all whom we find along the way to the manger.

To believe in God is always countercultural; to love all peoples is countercultural. Unfortunately, our culture has affected the way we carry out our personal relationships and has led us to a new place of fear and suspicion of the other. We no longer stop to help those on the roadside, we no longer give to beggars, we no longer ask for forgiveness, we no longer seek to make friends, we no longer want to learn another language, and we no longer want to hear the stories of others.

Sometimes we feel abandoned, lost, deceived, brokenhearted, and hopeless. Our story might not be one where things work out well, but on closer examination we, like Ruth, see more blessings than we realize. Ruth seeks to accompany Naomi because Naomi's faith has influenced her life. By her example, Ruth finds it fit to follow her.

Have we ever asked ourselves what makes us attractive to others? How do we invite people to join us on the journey of faith? How do we listen to those who admire or dislike us? We often forget that the Christian life is about friendship. Friendship with God and friendship with each other is what the spiritual journey is all about.

A Jesuit friend of mine used to say that spiritual conversation is the best way to deepen prayer, friendship with God, and friendship with other Christians. Conversation is shared with friends. Who are our friends? Who are our spiritual friends? What do we talk about with our friends? What do we talk about with spiritual friends?

IN THE WOMB

The Child keeps inching toward the birth canal, turning slowly. Some mothers are aware of the precise moment when their children turn in the womb. There is something deliberate in the action of the Child as the time for birth draws closer. The relationship shared between Ruth and Naomi is as certain and deliberate as the Child journeying toward birth.

The extremely slow pace of the Child's movement toward the birth canal is a great lesson for us. God does not expect us to approach life with perpetual leaping and bounding, or to run at full speed toward spiritual things. God knows that we do not always have a sense of urgency about what really matters. There are moments when we are eager to nourish our growth in the Lord, but at times the weight of life bears down too heavily upon us.

Advent reminds us each year that we need to get going. Yes, the journey of commitment to and responsibility in and through Jesus continues. The Brazilian church and many churches in Latin America speak of their faith journey in terms of a struggle or battle. Their cry to energize the faithful is to say, *A luta continua*—"The struggle continues."

Like the Child in the womb, when our surroundings get tight, we are called slowly to inch our way toward birth. So many tragedies, so many hurts, so many disappointments, so many dark moments can make us think of giving up. This

Advent may be a time to take comfort in the slow, almost imperceptible movement that is part of the life process.

SPIRITUAL EXERCISE

 Reread the passage from Ruth. Close your eyes and imagine the darkness of the womb. Try to imagine how the Child must look and feel at this stage of his development. Feel the snugness of the womb, feel the tightness, listen to the pulsing of the blood and the beating of Mary's heart. Experience what it feels like for the Child to inch forward. Say, "Lord, when it gets tough, help me to keep believing in you."

For Today

❊ How can this Advent be a time of forming new friendships in our lives?

❊ Ask God for the strength to mend some of the broken relationships in your life.

❊ Remember that God seeks to deepen our connections with all peoples.

Advent 2: Friday

Emmanuel, show your glory within me,
and give me wisdom today.

Advent is a time for repentance, a time to reflect on death, a time to mourn, and a time to be open to God's love.

IN THE SCRIPTURES
2 Samuel 12:15–18a, 20–23

The LORD struck the child that Uriah's wife bore to David, and it became very ill. David therefore pleaded with God for the child; David fasted, and went in and lay all night on the ground. The elders of his house stood beside him, urging him to rise from the ground; but he would not, nor did he eat food with them. On the seventh day the child died. . . . Then David rose from the ground, washed, anointed himself, and changed his clothes. He went into the house of the LORD, and worshiped; he then went to his own house; and when he asked, they set food before him and he ate. Then his servants said to him, "What is this thing that you have done? You fasted and wept for the child while it was alive; but when the child died, you rose and ate food." He said, "While the child was still alive, I fasted and wept; for I said, 'Who knows? The LORD may be gracious to me, and the child may live.' But now he is dead; why should I fast? Can I bring him back again? I shall go to him, but he will not return to me."

God deals with David's sin. David reflects on his actions and he grows in appreciation of the consequences of his actions and how God is a God of life. We meet David as he struggles to understand suffering, pain, loss, and death. Where in Advent do we find time for repentance? The thought of doing penance puts dread in the heart of many of us. We tend to shy away from what this word implies. So much of our society focuses on perfection, leading us to believe that there is no need for penance.

We also tend to focus on the need of others to do penance—like David, we forget that the bell tolls for us. But just as sin is never about the other person, so also penance is never about the other person; it is always about us. To approach God always involves repentance. As uncomfortable as this may make us, there is no way around it. We come to God knowing that we are sinners saved by the mercy and grace of God. We must own that we are sinners; we must own that we are guilty of coveting, committing adultery and fornication, harboring resentment, feeding anger, and living selfish lives. Penance does not take away the struggle or the sin, but what it does is focus us on the path to redemption, mercy, and light. If we do not embrace our sin and penance, we will not embrace the grace, forgiveness, and joy. To know our sin is to know our strength and grace.

If penance scares us, death scares us even more. For whatever reason, we have given in to the expectation of being forever young, forever healthy, forever alive. When a woman is pregnant there is much rejoicing, but we forget how tentative and how close to death a pregnancy draws a woman and the child she bears. Most women have had to deal with miscarriages and problematic pregnancies. Unfortunately, death, like pain, is hardly ever spoken about. We hide our death and hide our pain, because these experiences hurt so much.

Advent is a call to identify with the harshness that life dishes out to so many. How do we identify, empathize, and join ourselves to the pain and death of others? David had to face his pain and suffering; many of us have also been faced with pain and suffering, but we have chosen to deny or ignore it. We have crazy family members, distant relatives on welfare, parents in nursing homes, and hurtful memories that we choose to deny and ignore.

Advent is also a time to be open to God's blessings. We shy away from pain and shy away from blessings. At the heart of human complexity beats a duality of experiences. Every blessing brings a cross. Every grace brings a disgrace. Every hope holds up a certain amount of despair. How we deal with the cross shows us how we will deal with blessings. How we deal with disgrace tells a lot about how we will deal with grace. How we open ourselves to hope shows our openness to despair. Blessings come in all shapes, sizes, and colors. We receive blessings every day: the ability to breathe, to think, to move, to smile, to cry, to see the sun, to hear the wind, to go to work, to go to school, and to have a community. Society has changed our appreciation of what is valuable, but we need to reclaim the simple (and grandiose) things that are blessings from God. We are swimming in an ocean of blessings, but most of us think the ocean is mere water.

IN THE WOMB

The Child is dropping down into Mary's pelvis, which causes her tremendous heaviness and more discomfort. Even babies delivered by C-section drop down, so this is a path for all of us. His own weight and the natural process of getting ready for birth demand this of him. Dropping down for us may be an experience of falling on our knees before God when something glorious or frightening happens in our life. Dropping down may be an experience of letting go of some of the power we have in life. Dropping down may be paying attention to the *weight* in our life—what saps our energy, what distracts us. Dropping down might be allowing the word of God to take us into a new place. If we do not drop down, we cannot be born.

Advent calls us to dislodge ourselves from the comfort zone as we prepare for new birth. For parents and friends who have lost loved ones and find this time painful, our stories are mirrored in the lives of people close to God's heart.

SPIRITUAL EXERCISE

Reread the passage from 2 Samuel. Close your eyes and imagine the darkness of the womb. Try to imagine how the Child must look and feel at this stage of his development. Feel the snugness of the womb, feel the tightness, then try to experience the *drop down.* Say, "Lord, show me where I need to let go" or "Show me where I need to *drop down.*"

For Today

✿ How can this Advent be a time of repentance?

✿ Ask God for the strength to face the suffering and pain around you.

✿ Remember that God seeks to have us face our sins and blessings.

Advent 2: Saturday

Emmanuel, show your glory within me,
and lead me into your presence today.

Advent is a time when unexpected things can happen, a time to spend more time with God, and a time to renew our belief in a God who accomplishes the impossible.

IN THE SCRIPTURES
Luke 1:5, 11–15, 18–20

> In the days of King Herod of Judea, there was a priest named Zechariah, who belonged to the priestly order of Abijah.... Then there appeared to him an angel of the Lord, standing at the right side of the altar of incense. When Zechariah saw him, he was terrified; and fear overwhelmed him. But the angel said to him, "Do not be afraid, Zechariah, for your prayer has been heard. Your wife Elizabeth will bear you a son, and you will name him John. You will have joy and gladness, and many will rejoice at his birth, for he will be great in the sight of the Lord."... Zechariah said to the angel, "How will I know that this is so? For I am an old man, and my wife is getting on in years." The angel replied, "I am Gabriel. I stand in the presence of God, and I have been sent to speak to you and to bring you this good news. But now, because you did not believe my words, which will be fulfilled in their time, you will become mute, unable to speak, until the day these things occur."

God enters into the life of Elizabeth and Zechariah in a miraculous way. Gabriel appears to Zechariah and his faith gets put to the test. What happens in the life of this couple prepares the way for the Messiah.

Elizabeth and Zechariah represent the piety of those who dedicate their whole life to God. They represent each of us in so many ways because we also attempt to dedicate our lives to God. Forming part of the priestly class, they grew old together in love and service to God. They probably held each other at night and discussed the blessings in their life, wondering about their childless state. Why had God not given them a child? As people of faith, they must have grappled with this difficult aspect of their life, but managed to remain open to God's surprise. They knew that God would bless them, but probably did not know how.

How many of us get resentful so easily when we feel that we have been faithful, but not blessed? How many of us feel that we have given everything to God and received nothing in return? How many of us think that the time has passed for God to fulfill promises? Eventually God fulfills Elizabeth and Zechariah's wish, confounding all they thought that God could do for them and all that could ever happen in their life. Gabriel appears and promises that even in their old age they would conceive and bear a son.

God can do many things in our lives and so can we. When we fail to live lives open to the unexpected, we can fall by the roadside, ending up in a hopeless rut. It is in being faithful and being priestly that we experience the blessings of God. It is true, God can bless us even in our unfaithfulness, but the gift of life can only happen in the midst of faithfulness.

How could we spend more time with God, and renew our belief in God? One way to renew our faith is to reexamine our baptismal commitment, to live out the things we profess with our lips. How do we live out love for each other and for God? Zechariah was in the temple when he experienced the awesome and awful power of God. How much time do we spend in church? How much time do we spend in prayer? It is the church and our prayer that give us the capacity to do all things in God and to have all of God's things done to us.

Let us seek to be open to God's surprises. Let us seek to live in the light, even if surrounded by darkness.

IN THE WOMB

 The Child's intestines are accumulating more waste products from the liver, pancreas, and gall bladder; they are getting ready to perform an important function outside the womb.

Advent calls us to a faithful following, but we cannot forget that any following of the Child involves a cross. Every follower of the Child has to embrace the cross, the unpleasant, painful, and frightening challenges of life. We all have to accumulate spiritual meconium, and we have to hold on to it for awhile. Doctors get very worried about the health of the unborn child if the meconium is released too early, because it could get into the child's lungs and cause serious problems.

Like Elizabeth and Zechariah, we have to hold on to the unpleasant or the unexpected things that form part of our lives. The time will come, on God's timetable, when we can let go of our meconium. But the best time is always after birth and never before. Advent asks of all of us not to give up too soon, not to let go of the cross, and to trust that the Child will lead us to a new place in which we will discover how embracing the cross can bring us more blessings than we could have imagined in the moment.

SPIRITUAL EXERCISE

Reread the passage from Luke. Close your eyes and imagine the darkness of the womb. Try to imagine how the Child must look and feel at this stage of his development. See the meconium accumulating within the intestines of the Child. As unpleasant as this image may be, try to stay with it.

Imagine something in your life that is unpleasant and ask God for the grace to help you see how it may lead you to new surprises in God. Say, "Lord, help me to know your grace is sufficient for me. Lord, show me why I need to hold on to this cross."

For Today

✻ How can this Advent be a time of spiritual surprises?

✻ Ask God for the grace to embrace the crosses in your life.

✻ Remember that God seeks us to trust in divine providence more than in our human understanding.

The Third Week of
Advent

OUR CALL
FROM GOD

Advent is a time for us to remember that we are called by God. We are created by God and called to participate in the mission of God. To know God is to know God in every human being and in every situation—or at least to try. As we journey toward Christmas, God invites us to look into our hearts and into the world around us and see where we can the signs of God's hope and life. Look around and see where God is calling us. If at the end of Advent, all we do is believe this promise to Jeremiah, then we are surely on the way to something:

> "Now I have put my words in your mouth.
> See, today I appoint you over nations
>   and over kingdoms,
>   to pluck up and to pull down,
>   to destroy and to overthrow,
>   to build and to plant." (Jeremiah 1:9–10)

THIS WEEK IN THE WOMB

The Child continues to grow longer; fat continues to accumulate, even though he grows more slowly. Mary's weight gain has probably peaked, and she is not going to get any bigger than her present weight. He has no functioning tear ducts and they will not function at birth. His first cries will be loud, but tearless. Because the Child has had the muscles to swallow nutrients in the amniotic fluid, waste materials continue to increase in his intestines. The umbilical cord carries approximately three hundred quarts of fluid to him each day. He is feeding and swallowing at an alarming rate because of his awareness that delivery approaches.

Advent 3: Sunday

Emmanuel, let your peace dwell within me,
and let me rejoice in you today.

Advent is a time to share life experiences with others, to pay attention to the movement of the Holy Spirit within us, and to give prophetic witness to the power of God.

IN THE SCRIPTURES
Luke 1:39–49

In those days Mary set out and went with haste to a Judean town in the hill country, where she entered the house of Zechariah and greeted Elizabeth. When Elizabeth heard Mary's greeting, the child leaped in her womb. And Elizabeth was filled with the Holy Spirit and exclaimed with a loud cry, "Blessed are you among women, and blessed is the fruit of your womb. And why has this happened to me, that the mother of my Lord comes to me? For as soon as I heard the sound of your greeting, the child in my womb leaped for joy. And blessed is she who believed that there would be a fulfillment of what was spoken to her by the Lord."
    And Mary said,
    "My soul magnifies the Lord,
        and my spirit rejoices in God my Savior,

for he has looked with favor
  on the lowliness of his servant.
Surely, from now on all generations will call me blessed;
  for the Mighty One has done great things for me,
  and holy is his name."

Mary goes to visit her cousin Elizabeth. Two women connected by blood find new connections through the power of the Holy Spirit working in their lives. Both have experienced the good and embarrassing news of God. Pregnancy came as a surprise interruption of their lives; they have a lot to laugh and cry about. Mary models Christian discipleship by being a neighbor to Elizabeth; Elizabeth models humility and divine awareness.

Years ago, when I received word that my first book had been accepted for publication, I called up my wife. "I have some good news," I told her. "What is it?" she asked.

"Well, I want to tell you in person, face to face." There was a transit strike on at the time and I remember walking home for miles and thinking how Mary must have journeyed toward Elizabeth with her own news, to tell her in person, face to face.

Christianity is primarily about movement toward the other. Jesus challenged his disciples over and over again to go out, in order for them to encounter others. Good news cannot be shared with others from the comfort of our homes or the soft pews of the church. Good news requires a journey to meet the other in the hill country.

In this story, we encounter Mary walking the talk. She put herself at great risk and inconvenience to go visit her cousin Elizabeth. As she greets Elizabeth, the child in Elizabeth's womb leaps for joy. When we share who we are with others, something happens first in the other and then in us. We are all giving birth to something all the time. Good or evil gets born in us and the people around us every second of every day. Sharing the birth events of our lives is one way of guaranteeing a community of support.

As Christians, we cannot survive unless we share the ups and downs of the journey. God does not get too interested in the wonderful time we are having in life. God is more interested in how we are able to share the frightening moments with those around us. The reverse is also true. God wants to know how we listen to those who are different, older, poorer, and frightened.

During this season of Advent, we approach Christmas in spirit and truth only if we pay close attention to the movement of the Holy Spirit within us. We may experience a joy and confirmation that tell us that we are on the right path, that we are making progress, and that God is pleased with our openness to the Spirit. But even desolation brings us a chance to encounter the Spirit of God. When our spiritual lives feel dry, when we sense a heavy spirit, the Holy Spirit calls us to check ourselves. During desolation, we might get a tremendous awareness of the things we need to pay attention to in our lives in order to remain open. How do we pay attention to the Holy Spirit's activities in our lives?

Now more than ever, Christians need to give prophetic witness to God's activities in the world. Christmas cries out for a new proclamation of what is of God and what is of Caesar. Look at all the traditions around us that trap us into celebrating Christmas as though we were pagans. Most of what parades as Christmas is idolatrous. Most of what gets called preparation for Christmas, in truth, is a denial of Christmas. Most of what demands our attention during this time calls us away from what it means to be born anew in God.

Mary begins her prophetic witness by stating that her soul magnifies the Lord. Do our souls magnify the Lord? Mary proclaims that her spirit rejoices because the One who is mighty has done great things for her. Today God continues to show mercy, to bring down the powerful, to lift up the lowly, to fill the hungry with good things, and to send the rich away empty (Luke 1:52–53). Do we think of God in these terms?

How do we grapple with these qualities of God during this season where so many have all they need, while many more die before their time for lack of life's basic needs?

IN THE WOMB

The Child's weight and height have increased only a little from last week, but fat continues to accumulate even though he grows more slowly. Watching a child grow is fascinating because the growth is imperceptible and yet obvious. Slowly Mary's stomach grows and slowly the Child within her womb grows: nothing is rushed and everything happens in its own order and rhythm.

Mary's skin is overstretched by this time, but she knows that her stomach will not get much bigger now, thankfully so. Mary may be pondering the miracle of everything happening at the right time and in its orderly fashion. Her womb and her whole body adapted to the presence of the life within her: changing and stretching her in ways she had never imagined possible.

One of the greatest lessons we can learn both from Mary and the Child is that quite frequently the spiritual path requires a determination and commitment to grow, especially at times when we wish things would be clearer and quicker. Do we pay attention to the things that grow slowly but surely in our lives?

Advent calls us to continuous growth, especially as Christmas approaches. We who believe in the Child look at life with threefold eyes of faith: one eye looks back at what God has done, another at what God is doing in the present moment, and a third on what God will do. To balance all three perspectives is not an easy task, but we are called to participate in the dance. As Christmas approaches, we are called to focus on what God is doing now. Look around: What is God doing in our lives? What is God doing in the world? Is the reign of God slowly spreading in our hearts and in the world?

Within the womb growth is slower at this time, but every inch and every gram have their importance. When growth happens slowly, what is our outlook toward life? When the living slows down, how do we respond?

SPIRITUAL EXERCISE

Reread the passage from Luke. Close your eyes and imagine the darkness of the womb. Try to imagine how the Child must look and feel at this stage of his development. Be as still as you possibly can as you focus your awareness on your breathing. Imagine that every inhalation is a gift of the Holy Spirit, and every exhalation is a release of your troubles. Practice this breathing exercise for a few moments.

Then imagine yourself in the womb, ready to be born, and picture the Holy Spirit filling you with light and grace. Say, "Lord, thank you for the gift of the Holy Spirit."

For Today

❋ How might you experience the power of the Holy Spirit more fully this Advent?

❋ Ask God to increase your knowledge of the Child through the Holy Spirit.

❋ Remember that Advent is about representing God's redemption in actions in the world.

Advent 3: Monday

Emmanuel, let your peace dwell within me,
and let me see your glory today.

Advent is a time to celebrate the fact that we are on holy ground, to know that God is with us, and to participate in God's acts of liberation.

IN THE SCRIPTURES
Exodus 3:1–8

Moses was keeping the flock of his father-in-law Jethro, the priest of Midian; he led his flock beyond the wilderness, and came to Horeb, the mountain of God. There the angel of the LORD appeared to him in a flame of fire out of a bush; he looked, and the bush was blazing, yet it was not consumed. Then Moses said, "I must turn aside and look at this great sight, and see why the bush is not burned up." When the LORD saw that he had turned aside to see, God called to him out of the bush, "Moses, Moses!" And he said, "Here I am." Then he said, "Come no closer! Remove the sandals from your feet, for the place on which you are standing is holy ground." He said further, "I am the God of your father, the God of Abraham, the God of Isaac, and the God of Jacob." And Moses hid his face, for he was afraid to look at God.

Then the LORD said, "I have observed the misery of my people who are in Egypt; I have heard their cry on account of their taskmasters. Indeed, I know their sufferings, and I have come down to deliver them from the Egyptians, and to bring them up out of that land to a good and broad land, a land flowing with milk and honey."

Moses experiences a theophany, an awesome and awful experience of the Creator God that forever changes him, his relationship with God and his worldview. God is the One who is—timeless. God is the One who sees suffering—compassionate. God is the One who liberates—savior. Moses experiences this awesome reality in the burning bush. On so many levels, the child in the womb is a burning bush experience, because while drawing life from the mother, the mother does not lose life—the mother, like the bush, is not consumed. We are on holy ground when we know that God is with us and we participate in God's acts of liberation.

"I am the Lord your God," God repeats throughout the Scriptures, claiming and reclaiming us as the people of God. To be God's people creates in us a sense of celebration because wherever we are, we are in the presence of God. To be on holy ground requires more than a passive act of standing still. God invites us to ground ourselves in holiness that grows out of an ongoing experience of who God is.

In the story, Moses turned toward God and attempted to draw closer. Moses turned aside to see more clearly. It is in the turning that we turn out right, turning to face God. Some of us pass by the burning bushes of our lives and never bother to turn. We get so busy that we run past the roses. We get so busy that we pass the wounded along the path. We move so fast that those who wish have no way of pointing out to us that we are standing on holy ground. Sometimes we feel we know ourselves and our surroundings so well, we have given up on anything good ever happening. We need to look for the burning bushes. We need to turn aside and see God aflame in the eyes of our brothers and sisters, especially those who are suffering. What is holy about the ground on which we find ourselves? What is burning in our lives?

Part of being on holy ground is accepting that we have received the gift of faith through others. God has been faithful to our ancestors and to our friends. To be on holy ground calls us to a place of thanksgiving for the saintly men and women who have inspired us on this journey of faith. When we think about ancestors and friends in the faith, we also think about the way our lives will influence a future generation.

Advent reminds us that the God we serve is with us, one like us, and present to us. At times nothing is more difficult than owning, sensing, and proclaiming that God is with us and one like us. Obviously, the Child has already been born, and so the Child is already with us. When we examine ourselves, we discover that we live as if the Child is really only born once a year and does not exist before Christmas Day.

God is never revealed without a mission. Every encounter with God calls for action. What kind of action? we may ask. God makes several things clear throughout the Scriptures: God lives, God loves, and God cares, especially for those who are in bondage to sin or oppressed by unjust systems.

Some years ago, theologians from Latin America brought us a new way of looking at God. Their work, reflection, and presence among the poor brought about a theology for the liberation of the poor. These theologians claimed that God has a preferential option for and love of the poor. People of all faiths criticized them, saying that God is not partial. Yet God does seem pretty partial in this encounter with Moses. God does seem concerned that people are suffering. God does initiate a process of liberation. Whatever our views may be about liberation theology, we have to face the fact that many in our cities and world are crying out to God. Do we care about those who suffer? Do we make concrete and sacrificial actions on behalf of the poor?

IN THE WOMB

 The Child in the womb has no functioning tear ducts. His first cries will be loud but tearless. I can imagine Mary having shed many a tear. She might well have cried tears of joy when she knew she was pregnant with the Savior of the world. She might have cried when Joseph finally embraced her and told her that all was understood, and she might have cried when she went to visit her cousin Elizabeth. The tears of Advent. I imagine that Mary, Zechariah, Joseph, and Elizabeth were all well acquainted with tears.

We get so used to our tears that we forget that in our earliest days we did not have them. Tear ducts mature a few days or weeks after birth. What a great lesson to take into Christmas. Where are our tears? When was the last time we cried? When was the last time we felt moved to tears in joy or pain?

Advent calls us to pay attention to the suffering and pain of others because sometimes people's pain is expressed without tears. If we are looking to see tears, we could miss the cry of anguish. Some of us miss the tears and unfortunately also miss the cries. To journey toward the manger requires that we stop along the way to dry the tears, respond to the cries and set the captives free. It is a hard task. But there is nothing in the Christmas story that speaks of ease.

SPIRITUAL EXERCISE

 Reread the passage from Exodus. Close your eyes and imagine the darkness of the womb. Try to imagine how the Child must look and feel at this stage of his development. Imagine as best you can your own experience in the womb.

Slowly cover your eyes with your hands. Think of the last time you cried. Stay with that experience. Return to thinking of the Child developing in the womb. Slowly say, "Lord, in my moment of tears teach me about you."

For Today
* How can this Advent be a more profound encounter with God?
* Ask God for the grace to see the burning bushes in your life.
* Remember that our suffering and that of others might not always be obvious.

Advent 3: Tuesday

Emmanuel, let your peace dwell within me,
and give me a spirit of goodness and justice today.

Advent is a time to reevaluate what we do in God's name, to examine our life of prayer, and to recommit to a relationship of obedience.

IN THE SCRIPTURES
Isaiah 1:14–20

Your new moons and your appointed festivals
  my soul hates; they have become a burden to me,
    I am weary of bearing them.
When you stretch out your hands,
  I will hide my eyes from you;
    even though you make many prayers,
I will not listen; your hands are full of blood.
Wash yourselves; make yourselves clean;
  remove the evil of your doings from before my eyes;
  cease to do evil, learn to do good;
  seek justice, rescue the oppressed,
  defend the orphan, plead for the widow.
Come now, let us argue it out, says the LORD:
  though your sins are like scarlet, they shall be like snow;
  though they are red like crimson,
    they shall become like wool.
If you are willing and obedient,
  you shall eat the good of the land;
  but if you refuse and rebel,
    you shall be devoured by the sword;
for the mouth of the LORD has spoken.

The prophet Isaiah proclaims God's dissatisfaction with the people's festivities, celebrations and prayers. God declares that the people's sinfulness and oppression cause them to remain alienated from goodness, mercy and freedom. God draws a comparison between the animals who recognize their owners and human beings who are ignorant of God as Creator.

If we were to stop and think about all the things done in the name of God, we would be shocked. If we were to stop and examine some of the ways we worship God, we might be scandalized. Much of what we do in the name of God has nothing to do with God. Much of what we say in the name of God has nothing to do with God.

Sometimes we choose not to examine—not to know—our actions because we are terrified that they may be revealed as mere acts of idolatry and not the supreme worship we think we offer.

A few years ago, a Jewish friend asked me why Christians were so focused on eggs and bunnies during Easter. Few of our children know the Easter story, and most adults spend no time explaining to them the blessings that come along with Easter. Christmas suffers even more than Easter in our consumer society. Stores and companies start touting Christmas shopping as early as June, and we all get into a frenzy about buying the right gift, without paying sufficient attention to the Giver of all good things.

Children in churches perform pageants geared toward making them participate in church and not toward understanding the power of the manger and its implications for life. We spend hours decorating our yards and houses and spend less and less time looking at the state of our hearts. Listen to God's words spoken through Isaiah, the prophet: "Your new moons and your appointed festivals my soul hates; they have become a burden to me, I am weary of bearing them" (1:14).

Advent is a time to reexamine our Christian journey. Jesuits try to do an *examen* every night. It is a form of prayer that focuses on one's thoughts, actions, and words throughout the day. In an *examen* we spend time looking over our day as a means of being aware of God's presence throughout the day and considering how we were present to God.

Most of us will not have the discipline to examine our lives every night. But if we do not examine our Christian life, we will short-change our relationship with God. During Advent, when Christians celebrate the beginning of the church's year, we would do well to reflect on our lives and make resolutions that take into account the approaching Christ.

The cradle is the cross and Advent is Lent—we have to turn back to God. God calls us into a new relationship built on a faithfulness and obedience. Gandhi once said that if Christians lived like the Christ they professed, he would be a Christian. Martin Luther King, Jr., from a Birmingham jail challenged Christian leaders to examine how they were supporting the dictates of a racist America. Where does our obedience to God's word rub us the wrong way? Where in our lives do we find contradictions to the will of God?

IN THE WOMB

The Child's intestines are fully developed, now capable of bowel movements outside the womb—another indication that birth is not far off. He continues to find life, nourishment, and protection through the placenta, the umbilical cord, and the womb itself. Inside the womb, he finds all that he needs. A friend of mine told me that her interpretation of Noah's ark is that it provided everything needed. Yet, she continued, it was a smelly, messy place during a confusing time, but the ark provided shelter from what was happening outside.

Bowel movements can be very unpleasant, but we would be in bad shape without them. The Child in the womb continues to feast, but his body is preparing for new movements. We can learn not to be afraid when waste material builds up around us or within us. Trust in God: relief is always within sight and reach.

SPIRITUAL EXERCISE

Reread the passage from Isaiah. Close your eyes and imagine the darkness of the womb. Try to imagine how the Child must look and feel at this stage of his development.

Gently recall a tragic or unhappy incident in your life. Spend time with this event, focusing on how it has changed your life. Are you a better person for it? Has this incident led to a deeper awareness of God's presence in your life? Slowly say, "Lord, help me to accept and learn from the unpleasant moments in my life."

For Today

* How can this Advent be a time of true worship and conversion?
* Ask God for the grace to see the sin or weakness in your life.
* Remember that God calls us to get real.

Advent 3: Wednesday

Emmanuel, let your peace dwell within me,
and teach me to speak your words today.

Advent is a time to be conscious of our vocation, to dialogue with God, and to prepare for the mission of God.

IN THE SCRIPTURES
Jeremiah 1:4–10

Now the word of the LORD came to me saying,
"Before I formed you in the womb I knew you,
and before you were born I consecrated you;
I appointed you a prophet to the nations."

Then I said, "Ah, Lord GOD! Truly I do not know how to
speak, for I am only a boy." But the LORD said to me,
   "Do not say, 'I am only a boy';
      for you shall go to all to whom I send you,
      and you shall speak whatever I command you.
   Do not be afraid of them,
      for I am with you to deliver you, says the LORD."
Then the LORD put out his hand and touched my mouth;
and the LORD said to me,
   "Now I have put my words in your mouth.
   See, today I appoint you over nations
   and over kingdoms,
      to pluck up and to pull down,
      to destroy and to overthrow,
      to build and to plant."

Jeremiah experiences God's call. God makes clear to Jeremiah
the nature of his vocation, and Jeremiah accepts what God is
calling him to be and do. It is noteworthy that Jeremiah tries
to resist the call, but God counters by detailing what Jeremiah
will need to do. God knows how terrified Jeremiah feels and
tells him, "Do not be afraid." God says this to Jeremiah
because God is the author of life and had consecrated
Jeremiah before he was born.

God calls all of humanity into action, and the action
requires focusing on God and the ways of God, who is the
author of life. Following God is a hard task. To follow, we
have to leave where we live. God's call forever demands a dis-
location. Throughout the Scriptures people experienced the
call of God as one that required the individual in question to
leave land, family, and friends. Leaving the comfortable is
what God asks of us all.

Today we are accustomed to using maps and getting direc-
tions before setting out on a journey. We want to feel safe, we
want to know how long the journey will take, what is the
quickest route, even what the weather conditions will be.
How unlike the experience of our ancestors in faith when

they were called by God—rarely was there a roadmap or a blueprint on the faith journey.

In the darkness of Advent I know how difficult it is to get up and pray in the mornings when I would rather stay in bed. Yet I also know how important it is for me to respond to the call of God to prayer. Without prayer, I easily sink into patterns of being that do not reflect God or my best self.

Following God involves getting out of bed to pray, being ready for detours, rest stops, roadblocks, and mystifying experiences that leave us wondering if we will ever arrive where we are going. Who knows what tomorrow will bring? Who knows if God will ask us to go to Nineveh? Who knows if God will send us to Samaria? Who knows if on the way to Bethlehem God will tell us to return to Nazareth? We do not like surprises. We want to know ahead of time. Yet God is so different from us. Everything in God is new, different, and surprising all the time.

We get married and we think it is a piece of cake. Then God asks us to make sacrifices and to let go of our self-constructed understanding of what it means to be in love. We want out. We join a church community and soon the pastor asks us to pledge, to teach Sunday school, or to chair a committee. We want out. We begin to work and suddenly we hate the job. We want out. Our children and parents do not act the way we would like. We want out.

Following the Child means that things will not always turn out right, and quite often we will have to turn around. We may even get lost. A vocation involves continuous turning—turning around, turning out, and turning toward God.

Looking at this passage from Jeremiah, we get a profound insight into what it means to dialogue with God. Jeremiah tells God why he feels inadequate. Youth. We all have that. We all have youth within us. Green. We are that. We are all green within us. Inexperience. We all have that. We all have inexperience within us. But it is only in dialogue that God assures us that we are known and loved. God knows that we

are young, green, and inexperienced. Eternal and unconditional Love looks beyond all this to the place where all these
things become necessary gifts for God to use. In dialogue
with God we discover how being a "youth" plays right into
the design of God. What aspect of our life do we need to proclaim to God? Lord, I am controlling, jealous, disorganized,
careless, fearful, lonely, addictive, vindictive, anal retentive,
crazy, brokenhearted, afraid, doubtful.

Jeremiah experienced a call to take on nations and kingdoms. On some levels, this is easier than taking on ourselves.
God calls us to be missionaries to ourselves, then to our families and friends, and then to the world. Sometimes the order
gets turned around—after all, it is God's mission—but there
is no way around mission itself. A great place to prepare for
our mission in and with God is to start with our baptism.
What are the pledges we made to God or the promises that
others made on our behalf? Our mission may well be to
believe firmly in God. Our mission may well be to resist
Satan and all his works. Our mission may well be to pray.
What is our mission? What is our mission in the church?
Where is God directing us to witness more concretely?

IN THE WOMB

The umbilical cord carries approximately three
hundred quarts of fluid to the Child each day. The
connections between Mary and the Child are best
illustrated by the umbilical cord. It carries most of the nutrients that the Child needs from his mother. What an important lesson to remember: since our conception we have been
fed. In our Sunday worship we gather around the bread and
wine as a reminder that we serve a God who wishes to feed us
constantly and in every way.

As we approach Christmas, we notice how the stores and
plazas advertise their understanding of Christmas: bright
lights, colorful decorations, sales, the latest clothes and gadg-
ets. We are fed constantly a need to buy, a need to lose our-

selves in continual stimulation. We are fed a diet of marvelous new inventions and designs, all intended to make us spend what we do not have or cannot afford. This is a great time to ask ourselves how we are being fed this Christmas. What gives us energy? What enriches our spiritual life? What feeds us a better understanding of the reason for the season?

How do we hear God's call? How do we receive "three hundred quarts" of fluid each day from God?

SPIRITUAL EXERCISE

 Reread the passage from Jeremiah. Close your eyes and imagine the darkness of the womb. Try to imagine how the Child must look and feel at this stage of his development. Meditate on the umbilical cord, watching the nutrients, the antibodies, the life flowing into the Child.

Then think of your experience within your mother's womb. Offer up thanksgiving for your mother and the time you were nurtured in the womb. Say, "Lord, keep me connected to you."

For Today

⁜ How can this Advent be a time of feeding on God's word and love?

⁜ Ask God to heal the places that are being fed by sin in your life.

⁜ Remember that God calls us to get connected to the mission and reign of God.

Advent 3: Thursday

Emmanuel, let your peace dwell within me,
and remind me how wonderfully made I am today.

Advent is a time to know that God is near to us, a time to accept God's care, and a time to grapple with the thoughts of God.

IN THE SCRIPTURES
Psalm 139:1–4, 13–16

> O LORD, you have searched me and known me.
> You know when I sit down and when I rise up;
>   you discern my thoughts from far away.
> You search out my path and my lying down,
>   and are acquainted with all my ways.
> Even before a word is on my tongue,
>   O LORD, you know it completely. . . .
> For it was you who formed my inward parts;
>   you knit me together in my mother's womb.
> I praise you, for I am fearfully and wonderfully made.
> Wonderful are your works; that I know very well.
> My frame was not hidden from you,
>   when I was being made in secret,
>   intricately woven in the depths of the earth.
> Your eyes beheld my unformed substance.
> In your book were written
>   all the days that were formed for me,
> when none of them as yet existed.

The psalmist celebrates God's presence that touches and knows every aspect of his life, even at the moment of conception. Surrendering to God's knowledge and marveling at

God's omnipresence, the psalmist offers every aspect of his life to God in prayer. His prayer touches all the bases of his relationship with himself and God. He thanks God, asks for forgiveness, petitions for his needs, and adores God.

"I in them and you in me" (John 17:23) is how Jesus describes the relationship among his followers, himself, and his Father. Listening to the news and looking at the reality around us does not show, on the surface, that God is near. More and more people lose their jobs and benefits; violence is on the rise; an increasing number of our family and friends contract frightening illnesses; the news is full of famines, wars, and natural disasters throughout the world. It is very hard to claim that God is near, because the signs are not that obvious. Looking at these realities with the eyes of faith, however, we see and interpret them differently. Amid the confusion, pain, and suffering, we believe God is at work in the world to bring about good.

As a Jesuit missionary, I spent a lot of time doing missionary work in the jungles of Brazil and Guyana. It never ceased to amaze me that in the homes of the humblest and poorest people I would always find three things: a table of hospitality, an altar, and music. Word spread easily and quickly that the priest was on his way, but I was always astounded at how quickly every family I visited was able to find coffee, bread and butter, and, quite frequently, beer. Then when we gathered as a community we always shared a feast with chicken, beef, and rice and peas.

I soon learned how to thank them for their gifts: by eating as much as possible. With the little that they had, they were happy to feed the priest. This act of giving was a concrete way they could express their thanks to God. One day, when I asked why they gave me so much food, an old lady with no teeth in her mouth laughed and said, "We are not feeding you! We are feeding God."

Advent invites us to grapple with the thoughts of God. What does God think? What would God think? We put so much emphasis on God's actions that we forget to focus on the thoughts of God. We have to admit that when we speak of God's action and thoughts, we are not quite sure what we are talking about. If we view God's thoughts as God's consciousness, we can better understand that God is present and forever thinking. God thinks through our easy moments, thinks through our difficult moments, and thinks along with the events that happen in our lives and in the world. One of the tasks of Christianity that we quite frequently forget is to seek to take on the mind and thoughts of Christ. There is an old saying that goes, "Think before you leap." This adage calls us to think before we act. As Christians, we need to reclaim an attitude of thinking in and with God before we act. Hopefully, the more we think *with* God, the more we will think and act *like* God.

IN THE WOMB

The Child is feeding and swallowing at an alarming rate. Within the womb, the Child knows instinctively that delivery approaches and so this increased feeding is in preparation for life on the outside. The Child's constant feeding must have left Mary feeling even more exhausted, but I wonder, as she rubbed her hand over her stomach, if she did not think of Psalm 139: "For it was you who formed my inward parts; you knit me together in my mother's womb. I praise you, for I am fearfully and wonderfully made."

Every moment of the pregnancy has been filled with activities that will lead to a healthy child, but Mary feels the results of the life within her. Exhausted and fatigued, did she feel inclined to pray?

Many of us experience a lack of energy and loss of motivation around this time of year. For some of us, it is just the fatigue and anxiety that comes from the ending of the year; for others, it is the change in weather.

The Jesuits have a saying of their own to counteract the feeling of lethargy in the spiritual life: *agere contra*. It means to go against the feeling. If the desire at this time is to overeat, fast. If the desire at this time is to stay in bed, rise early. If the inclination at this time is to gossip or complain, keep silent. In short, this is a spiritual practice of countering any negative activity with a positive or the opposite action. The Child keeps eating, keeps feeding; Advent calls us to keep feeding on God, to keep making the sacrifices that make us more aware of God's actions in our lives.

SPIRITUAL EXERCISE

Reread Psalm 139. Close your eyes and imagine the darkness of the womb. Try to imagine how the Child must look and feel at this stage of his development. Meditate on the Child feeding in his mother's womb. Pay attention to the small jaws of the Child doing what they must to keep him alive and healthy. Focus on the heart as it beats and on the undivided attention the Child pays to the feeding process.

Offer up a prayer of thanksgiving for your life. Thank God for all your actions, thoughts, desires, and everything about your life, whether positive or negative. Say, "Lord, thank you for nurturing me," or "Keep me focused on your coming."

For Today

❊ How can this Advent be a time of surrendering to God's knowledge of who you are?

❊ Ask God to search those areas of your life where you feel distanced from God.

❊ Remember that you are wonderfully made and that God thinks of you daily.

Advent 3: Friday

Emmanuel, let your peace dwell within me,
and remind me that you pay attention to my heart today.

Advent is a time to remember that at times God chooses those on the margins, those who are not present.

IN THE SCRIPTURES
1 Samuel 16:1, 6–7, 10–13

The LORD said to Samuel, "How long will you grieve over Saul? I have rejected him from being king over Israel. Fill your horn with oil and set out; I will send you to Jesse the Bethlehemite, for I have provided for myself a king among his sons."... When [the sons of Jesse] came, he looked on Eliab and thought, "Surely the LORD's anointed is now before the LORD." But the LORD said to Samuel, "Do not look on his appearance or on the height of his stature, because I have rejected him; for the LORD does not see as mortals see; they look on the outward appearance, but the LORD looks on the heart."...

Jesse made seven of his sons pass before Samuel, and Samuel said to Jesse, "The LORD has not chosen any of these." Samuel said to Jesse, "Are all your sons here?" And he said, "There remains yet the youngest, but he is keeping the sheep." And Samuel said to Jesse, "Send and bring him; for we will not sit down until he comes here." He sent and brought him in. Now he was ruddy, and had beautiful eyes, and was handsome. The LORD said, "Rise and anoint him; for this is the one." Then Samuel took the horn of oil, and anointed him in the presence of his brothers; and the spirit of the LORD came mightily upon David from that day forward.

Samuel learns an important lesson about the ways of God. God chooses David after rejecting seven of Jesse's sons, who all appeared to have qualities fit for a king, but not the king that God wanted. This passage of Scripture is quite intriguing for its treatment of God's rejection of Saul, and God's views of human qualities.

In this passage we see that there are indeed things that God rejects and things that God chooses. At times God chooses those on the margins, those not present. God rejects the projects of our hearts and actions that bring pain, alienation, and death to ourselves and others. "So, because you are lukewarm, and neither cold nor hot, I am about to spit you out of my mouth" (Revelation 3:16). It seems there is a growing appetite among us to accept all things and reject nothing. Some of this confusion comes from our attempts to love inclusively as God does. In our attempts to imitate God, we rightfully get confused about what, if anything or anyone, can be rejected by God.

There is no easy answer to this dilemma about whether God rejects individuals or things we love. It is fair to assume that there are some actions and some people that displease God. When we hurt others, when we choose to live in fear, when we choose to carry resentment, we can bet our bottom dollar that God rejects these actions. When corporations oppress their employees, when governments favor the wealthy over the poor, and when institutions turn a blind eye to those who are in need of help, we can be sure that God rejects these actions. The God we serve is a God of life, and anything that leads to death, God rejects.

In choosing to have a king, the people of Israel chose not to believe completely in God's ability to lead them and protect them. King Saul soon imitated the people he was elected to rule; he soon stopped believing that God could lead and protect him. And so God rejected him. God rejects our attempts to hold on to the trappings of life that do not bring life. God rejects our vain attempts to direct our lives independently of God's love and words. God rejects our attempts to be powerful and to control our destiny. Any turning away from God is rejected by God, because when we turn away from God we turn toward death.

Advent calls us to remember that there are things that God chooses. We tend to refuse the things that we should choose and choose the things that we should refuse. To choose and refuse like God requires that we pay attention to God. Choosing like God is a task of ongoing discernment in the spiritual life. Out of love, God chose to send the Child. God chose to be born of a poor, young, virgin girl. God chose not to control the events around the birth of the Child, and so the Child was born in a dirty manger. The things God chooses do not seem to mirror the things we choose. Quite frequently, God's choices do not make much sense to us, from our human point of view.

Advent presents us with the opportunity to see God working on the margins of our lives. Jesse's sons must have gathered before Samuel, each thinking that either he or one of the brothers in the room would be chosen king. Not one of them thought that their shepherd brother would be the one chosen by God. David was out of sight and out of mind, because they thought they were adequate and sufficient. Not one of them remembered him.

What aspects of our lives have we forgotten or tried to forget, and why? Who are the people we have forgotten? Sometimes the king God seeks is out in the field. What a great lesson to remember at Advent, that God is calling us to remember those outside. It would shock many of us to have God come visit our homes, offices, or churches and choose the *ugly duckling*. "Are all your sons here?" Samuel asks Jesse. God asks us if all our marbles—our thoughts, hopes, dreams, friends, desires, and even sins—are here. At some point, we will have to call in those things or people keeping sheep outside our hearts, homes, experiences, and church.

IN THE WOMB

The Child is shedding dead skin, along with the shedding of the protective hair from his body. He naturally rejects all the skin cells and protective hair that are not necessary for further growth. This action is not all that different from what we experience on a daily basis: we too shed dead skin without noticing it. Letting go, shedding, rejecting, and changing all form part of the natural events of life.

What happens in the womb can help teach us about letting go and rejecting the areas of our lives that do not contribute to our growth. Life is about letting go and holding on; accepting and rejecting.

Advent leads us toward God, and as we journey we discover that there are many things we need to put down, give up, or throw down. We do this because those who journey discover that some things are no longer necessary. Most of us spend time deciding what to choose and refuse. Many of us choose to keep the over-packed suitcases instead of parting with anything. What are the activities we do at this time of the year that are waste or mere waste of time? We cannot hold on to everything we have been given—nor should we.

How do we let go of hurt this Advent? How do we let go of infantile views of God? How do we let go of childish interpretations of Scripture? How do we let go of an old way of relating to each other and to God?

SPIRITUAL EXERCISE

Reread the passage from 1 Samuel. Close your eyes and imagine the darkness of the womb. Try to imagine how the Child must look and feel at this stage of his development. Imagine that you are on a journey to meet the Christ Child. Before you leave, pack your bags and pack the Child a gift. What would you take? What do you need along the journey? What gift would you bring to the Child?

If you have ever climbed a mountain or walked for a long distance, imagine that you are making the journey with what you packed. Then imagine that halfway along the journey you are told that you can only bring one thing for yourself and one thing for the Child. Pay attention to the items as you go through them. What do you choose to take and why? Slowly say, "Lord, give me a discerning heart" or "Lord, help to choose correctly."

For Today

❉ How can this Advent be a time of choosing the things and ways of God?

❉ Ask God for the gift to be faithful and open to the things of God.

❉ Remember that God pays attention to the things on the margins of our lives.

Advent 3: Saturday

Emmanuel, let your peace dwell within me,
and look favorably on me today.

Advent is a time to experience the fulfillment of God's words, to relish the promises of God, and a time to grow strong in spirit.

IN THE SCRIPTURES
Luke 1:57–64

Now the time came for Elizabeth to give birth, and she bore a son. Her neighbors and relatives heard that the Lord had shown his great mercy to her, and they rejoiced with her.

On the eighth day they came to circumcise the child, and they were going to name him Zechariah after his father.

But his mother said, "No; he is to be called John." They said to her, "None of your relatives has this name." Then they began motioning to his father to find out what name he wanted to give him. He asked for a writing tablet and wrote, "His name is John." And all of them were amazed. Immediately his mouth was opened and his tongue freed, and he began to speak, praising God.

Elizabeth gives birth, fulfilling the promise of the angel, and there is great rejoicing. Everything happens according to the word of the angel Gabriel: a child born to the aged couple, Zechariah speaks, and names his son John. Zechariah then goes on to prophesy about God's faithfulness and the role his son will play in the history of salvation.

The Scriptures tell us over and over again that "all things work together for good for those who love God" (Romans 8:28). The creation story in Genesis challenges us to believe in the power of God's word. God speaks and things come to pass. In the same way, God's words seek fulfillment in our hearts and lives. We sometimes can distance ourselves from the power of the Scriptures, either because of our lack of faith, or because we do not wish to deepen our understanding of what they have to say to us.

Elizabeth and Zechariah must have felt foolish believing that what God said would happen. Even with the loss of speech, Zechariah must have wondered if he was dreaming. Many pregnant mothers have said that even well into their pregnancy, they still cannot believe they are pregnant. This couple reminds us of the awesomeness of God's power and God's ability to do what most of us would consider totally impossible.

Would we even entertain the possibility of giving life when we know or feel that we are beyond the stage when it is possible? Can we believe that God can open us to a fruitful and glorious living of the gospel? Can we believe that God can call us into something new and exciting, even though we are small, insignificant, and incapable? Advent is truly a time to believe. We are called to believe that death is not the final word. We are called to believe that love is always most important. We are called to believe that God cares for us and works wonders in our lives every single day.

As Christmas draws nearer, we must remember that it is a fulfillment of God's word. Indeed, this is what we celebrate, "The Word became flesh." God's word seeks an embodiment in us. Notice how happy neighbors tried to convince Zechariah and Elizabeth of a different way of doing things, a way contrary to what God had said. To experience the fulfillment of God's words, we have to be resolute even when the blessings come. We have to name the child John. Who knows why God chose that name? But what Zechariah and Elizabeth knew was that it was the wish of God. We are called to fulfill that promise by living our lives according to the wishes of God. Listen to the words of Zechariah:

> And you, child, will be called the
>   prophet of the Most High;
> for you will go before the Lord
>   to prepare his ways,
> to give knowledge of salvation to his people
>   by the forgiveness of their sins.
> By the tender mercy of our God,
>   the dawn from on high will break upon us,
> to give light to those who sit in darkness
>   and in the shadow of death,
>   to guide our feet into the way of peace.
>   (Luke 1:76–79)

Today many Christians live either in a state of panic or downright disbelief. We panic because things do not seem to be working out the way we think they should. Or we really do not believe that God makes much of a difference, and sticking to the promises of God is being superstitious. Advent affords us a chance to pay attention to what we truly believe about God's promises. God calls us simply to be prayerful, wherever we find ourselves on the spectrum of belief in God's promises. God is faithful. God is real. God wants us to struggle honestly with God, the way Jacob struggled with the angel.

Advent is a time to grow strong in the spirit. John the Baptist went into the desert as a way of fortifying his spirit. Would to God we were able to retreat from this maddening world at times and go into the desert. In many ways, we do not have the luxury of John to retreat into a desert, but there are other forms of desert places. We cannot be mature Christians without passing through the deserts of disappointment, death, hurt, pain, and suffering. Yes, we all have our deserts to face. To grow strong in the spirit will demand that we be tested over and over again. Quite frequently, we opt not to grow in spirit; we do not rock the boat of our lives. God is calling us to grow. The quicker we realize that every stage of development requires some amount of pain, the sooner we will go into the desert and seek growth. Praying is one way of entering the desert and growing in the spirit. Seeking forgiveness and forgiving others is another way of entering the desert and seeking growth. Seeking to have the Child be born anew in us is one way of growing strong in the spirit.

IN THE WOMB

 A week before the Child is born, his testicles drop down into the scrotum. He is male, and this is what happens to every male child. Advent stands as the supreme invitation for Christians to deepen who we profess to be. How are we growing into the people God has created us to be? We are Christians; what is it that should happen to us as Christmas approaches? Indeed, this is the question that we need to answer. How do we demonstrate what it means to be the people of God?

Hopefully, at this stage we are satisfied with our sexual identities. And even this is more difficult than most of us will let on. Men and women continue to misunderstand each other and miscommunicate. The same is true for relations among men and among women. Advent is a time to examine our many relationships and the responsibilities we have to sustain them and give them life.

How do we become the Christians God wants us to be? How do we live more deeply into who God is calling us to be? How do we become more holy? How do we become more centered on God? These are Advent questions, and our celebration of Christmas will have more meaning for us if we seek to answer them.

SPIRITUAL EXERCISE

 Reread the passage from Luke. Close your eyes and imagine the darkness of the womb. Try to imagine how the Child must look and feel at this stage of his development.

Now imagine that you were one of the neighbors present at the public celebration of the birth of John. Listen to what the people are saying. Notice what you are feeling and notice what Elizabeth and Zechariah are doing. Pay special attention to Zechariah. Imagine that you are the one who offers him something to write on. Say, "Lord, let me glorify your name" or "Lord, help me to believe in your promises."

For Today

　　❊ How can this Advent be a time of staying faithful to
　　　God's words for you?

　　❊ Ask God for the gift of prophecy, or eyes to see how
　　　God is at work in the world.

　　❊ Remember that God is faithful and calls you to faith-
　　　fulness.

The Fourth Week of
Advent

GOOD NEWS
AND LIGHT

Advent is truly a time to hear the good news of God and to experience the light of Christ. This good news creates in us a desire to live our lives to the fullest and in the best way possible. Good news by its very nature demands to be shared. Jesus proclaimed that he is the light of the world and those who walk in him would have the light of light. Hopefully, this Advent will find us more eager to walk in the light as children of the light that shines in the darkness: "What has come into being in him was life, and the life was the light of all people. The light shines in the darkness, and the darkness did not overcome it" (John 1:3–5).

THIS WEEK IN THE WOMB

The Child is ready to be born any time this week, ready to come into the world. He still gains weight and is even more aware of light, sound, and the activities of his mother's body. Most of the vernix—the creamy protective substance on his body—that covered the Child has fallen off. Five unconnected bony plates will provide his skull with a changing shape to ease delivery. His gums are ridged, as if teeth are ready to emerge. His color is blue, purplish, yellowish white, or bluish pink due to the growing layer of fat. The Child receives a temporary supply of disease-combating antibodies, and these will protect him from viruses and sicknesses that can cause illness in newborns. His first breath will be the hardest thing he has done up to this point in his life. He will give a mighty gasp and scream as a way of filling up the thousands of air sacs in the lungs.

Advent 4: Sunday

O come, O come Emmanuel,
and live within my heart, soul, and mind today.

Advent is a time for conversion, a time to choose the light, and a time to live as beloved children of God.

IN THE SCRIPTURES
John 1:1–14

In the beginning was the Word, and the Word was with God, and the Word was God. He was in the beginning with God. All things came into being through him, and without him not one thing came into being. What has come into being in him was life, and the life was the light of all people. The light shines in the darkness, and the darkness did not overcome it.

There was a man sent from God, whose name was John. He came as a witness to testify to the light, so that all might believe through him. He himself was not the light, but he came to testify to the light. The true light, which enlightens everyone, was coming into the world.

He was in the world, and the world came into being through him; yet the world did not know him. He came to what was his own, and his own people did not accept him. But to all who received him, who believed in his name, he gave power to become children of God, who were born, not of blood or of the will of the flesh or of the will of man, but of God.

And the Word became flesh and lived among us, and we have seen his glory, the glory as of a father's only son, full of grace and truth.

The Gospel of John opens with one of the most powerful and poetic passages of Scripture. Celebrating God's self-revelation to the world through the Word, the writer professes belief in the Child Christ as God incarnate, through whom all things move and have their being. Years ago, I found myself struggling trying to figure out what this passage meant. I read and reread it, prayed over it, and thought about it for a long time. Then I began to see it as a nativity story and started to read it at the beginning of every Advent.

The first Advent after my son's birth, it dawned on me that the best way to understand the passage from John was to try to explain it to my son. So I kept reading it to him: just enjoying the poetry of it, reading and rereading it for its own sake. Then I wrote a children's book about this passage called *Jesus, the Word.* As I worked on making sense of it for a younger reader, one thing became clear: John wanted the reader to know that God loved the world, that Jesus' entry into the world was designed to make the world a better place, and that God would forever be involved in the world in concrete ways because of the incarnation. Here is how I ended up paraphrasing John's prologue:

And the Word of God
Won't let me be
Anything but holy, good, and free.

How would you communicate some of the truth that John wanted his readers to learn?

The weeks before Christmas are a time for ongoing conversion. They offer us days in which to learn how to choose the light, to live as children of God. "I have come to call not the righteous but sinners" (Matthew 9:13). When Jesus spoke these words, he was being verbally attacked for spending time with prostitutes, tax collectors, and other "low life" in that society. Those who spoke against his actions clearly believed that they were above these people, whom they thought were beyond the point of conversion, beyond the reach of God's love. Why do we believe that other people's sins are unforgivable?

Many of us would gladly identify with the righteous. Even when we do admit our faults, we go to great lengths to explain why ours are different. And of course, we are better than those on welfare, those who are unemployed or in bad marriages, those who never finish school, those who have bad credit. We are certainly better than those who do not go to church, aren't we?

If we allow the Lord to enlighten our darkness, we soon discover that we are no different from those we condemn. Sometimes we jump to condemn others simply as a means of taking the attention away from ourselves.

We can choose the light. Choosing the good and the light is not always an easy process. Many give up on growth in the Christian life because they find it difficult to shake their destructive patterns of behavior. We have learned we should choose the good, but we do not always understand the role of desire. If we do not understand desire, we will never understand choice. Desire is what saves us in the Christian life.

Desire is an innate gift of the Holy Spirit that needs to be intentionally cultivated. Desiring to do good, even when we do not choose to, is a step in the right direction. Let us be patient with ourselves when we fail to pray, fail to be courageous, or fail to practice what we preach. Let us tap into our gift of desire and cultivate it though prayer.

Advent invites us to stand up as children of God. Being children, of course, requires having birth parents, and this is the rub. Some of us do not treasure the time spent with our parents or do not have parents at all. Because of this, we find it hard to understand what it means to have God as our parent and to be children of God. On the other hand, some of us have had wonderful relationships with our parents, and it is easy for us to understand God as loving parent. In Christian community, we can share our experiences of childhood and explore our understandings of God as parent. When was the last time we shared our experiences as parents and children in a faith setting? When was the last time we shared the joys and pains of our childhood in the context of a prayer gathering or Eucharist? Doing this could be a tremendous source of healing and life this Advent.

Being children of God requires that we act like children. Cry when you need milk. Act silly to make God laugh. Listen to what God says. Throw things off the table and experience God's patience. Curl up in the arms of God. Ask God to read you a story. Allow God to throw you up in the air. Play hide and seek with God. Allow God to play hide and seek with you. Cry when God goes away. Squeal with delight when God comes back. Listen to God say how much you are loved. Tell God of your love. This, without a doubt, is what Advent is all about.

IN THE WOMB

 The Child is fully formed and is full-term, and ready to come into the world. Mary, who is often described as the first disciple, knows now the full weight of pregnancy. Imagine the heaviness of Mary's womb, as she journeys and searches for a place to bear her Child, thinking that the day of delivery would never come.

There is a saying in Jamaica, where I grew up: It is not what you carry, but how well you carry it. Pregnant women, especially those who go full-term, will tell you that even though the weight of pregnancy limits them and weighs them down, quite frequently the joy of the pregnancy and the joy to come makes their burden light. The weight of the womb frequently seems unbearable, but pregnant women focus on what is to come and recognize how connected they are to what is within them. They remember when there was hardly any weight to the fetus, and they remember the slow growth and the increasing weight.

The experience of women in the last week of pregnancy or right before the birth of a child reminds us all of the importance of bearing our burdens well. We all think that our own burden is the heaviest, and fail to think that the burden could well lead to a new life. Advent is a wonderful season that can remind us that the burdens of our lives can lead us to new and wonderful places filled with joy, peace, and hope.

When being a Christian becomes a burden, may we recognize that it is part of being a disciple, part of being faithful to God. May we have the grace to hear God's call through Jesus: "Come to me, all you that are weary and are carrying heavy burdens" (Matthew 11:28).

SPIRITUAL EXERCISE

Reread the passage from John. Close your eyes and imagine the darkness of the womb. Try to imagine how the Child must look and feel at this stage of his development. Imagine the Child getting ready for the world. He is not to be born yet, but he is almost there. Stay with this sense of impending birth. Then imagine that Mary invites you to place your hand or head on her stomach to feel the Child moving. Notice what it feels like to touch her stomach and feel the Child moving.

Pray for the grace to be "ready for the world." Say, "Lord, clothe me in your armor," or "Lord, prepare me to be a sanctuary."

For Today

※ How can this Advent be a time of readiness for the world?

※ Ask God for the gift of a converted heart.

※ Remember that the Child is the Word and the Light that has come into the world.

Advent 4: Monday

O come, O come Emmanuel,
and journey with me along the way today.

Advent is a time to pay attention to what is happening in our world, to be willing to head toward Bethlehem.

IN THE SCRIPTURES
Luke 2:1–5

> In those days a decree went out from Emperor Augustus that all the world should be registered. This was the first registration and was taken while Quirinius was governor of Syria. All went to their own towns to be registered. Joseph also went from the town of Nazareth in Galilee to Judea, to the city of David called Bethlehem, because he was descended from the house and family of David. He went to be registered with Mary, to whom he was engaged and who was expecting a child.

Luke shows the power of the emperor and contrasts it with the helplessness of the Child and his parents who must obey the decree. Luke seeks to show that the Child was born in the town of David, the great king.

So much trouble is happening in our world. The powers of this world have conspired to oppress, deceive, and lead many astray, all under the guise of doing what is best for us. "If the world hates you, be aware that it hated me before it hated you" (John 15:18). Do we really feel confident in our government's ability to make the world a better and holier place? Maybe we do, and maybe we do not. Either way, we are called to ask ourselves whether being a people of God makes a difference in the world at all.

In Advent we examine our willingness to move (or to be moved) to a posture of responsiveness. Of course, there are moments in life when what we need more than anything else is to stay put. In matters of social justice, Christian responsibility, mercy, and compassion, may we be unwavering in our commitment. Similarly, in matters of love, faith, and forgiveness, may God find us firm and immovable as a rock. And yet, there are times in life when we must move. Examining the Scriptures, we see the Spirit of God initiating growth and change in the lives of believers. Over and over again, those who believed in God received a call to leave land, family, and the known for a new destination. And they moved in faith. Quite often the call to move was about desire, inviting believers to change their heart's desires in obedience to the will of God. How can we turn our hearts over to the Holy Spirit today? How do we get out of the way today?

Sometimes when we move in the direction of God's will, it may seem that we are responding to other forces or circumstances in our lives. But we must never forget that God moves in mysterious ways, the wonders of God to perform. Looking at Joseph and Mary and trying to imitate them can teach us a lot about the way in which God calls us to move, or the way God makes our turnings turn out right. Nazareth means the "town of bread," and Bethlehem the "town of peace." The symbolic move from bread to peace is interesting to consider. We may be tempted to stay with bread, to feast on bread alone. But God calls us from the place where we feast to a place of peace. Mary and Joseph make this journey in what must have been a most precarious time. I wonder if they even doubted they could make it.

Obviously, Luke wants us to make the connection between the Child and King David, and we should. Yet there is something deeper and more beautiful in the story of this couple, so advanced in pregnancy and following the decrees of the emperor. There are times when obedience to the laws of government is exactly what God wants of us. When these laws are just, we can find God's providence all along the way, not only at the end of the journey. Let us move with Mary and Joseph, even as we, too, may wonder if we can make it.

IN THE WOMB

There is not much space in the womb now; the Child does not have much wiggle room. The beautiful womb is filled. In these final days before birth the tight quarters mean a decline in fetal movement, but we can be sure that the Child, like all other children, is still capable of a few good kicks.

One of my favorite Taizé songs is: "Come and fill our hearts with your peace, you alone, O Lord, are holy." Whenever Advent comes around, I think of this song, because Mary was filled with the peace of God by bearing the Prince of Peace. I also think of the many times that I could not feel God's presence in my life, but when I took the time to be still and reflect, I always discovered that God was there, deep within. In the stillness I could find God.

One of the greatest temptations we face as human beings is to begin to doubt that there is life when things are quiet. The Child in the womb reminds us that though things may be quiet, life is still growing. My wife had an interesting reaction during the last few days of her pregnancy. Because we had had a problematic pregnancy, whenever the womb was quiet and there was no perceptible movement, Kathy got very worried. However, she had developed wonderful ways of communicating with our son in the womb. She would start singing and stroking her stomach—and sure enough, she would feel a kick. The quiet child in a tight place knew that she wanted to be sure he was all right.

When we are filled with God's Spirit and even in those times when we are filled with distractions, the life of God still resides deep within us, and if we are still and if we pay attention we discover the stirrings of God. Everything is full of God's glory. Imagine Mary filled not only with the Holy

Spirit, but filled with a physical reality that was actually the living Word of God.

SPIRITUAL EXERCISE

Reread the passage from Luke. Close your eyes and imagine the darkness of the womb. Try to imagine how the Child must look and feel at this stage of his development. Then imagine that you are walking with Mary and Joseph as they journey toward Bethlehem. Pay attention to Mary as she winces and groans when the pregnancy is hard to bear and the journey feels too long. How do you respond to her pain? Picture yourself having a conversation with Joseph. What do you ask him? What does he say? Then picture yourself saying good-bye once you arrive in Bethlehem.

Pray for the grace to be compassionate to those you meet along the journey of faith. Say, "Lord, I want to walk with you," or "Lord, preserve my spirit."

For Today

   ❊ How can this Advent be a time of movement from fear to life?

   ❊ Ask God to shepherd your path and to enlighten your heart.

   ❊ Remember that God is always leading you toward peace.

Advent 4: Tuesday

O come, O come Emmanuel,
and fill my heart with your love today.

Advent is a time to remember God's unconditional love for us, to remember that we are called to love others and that love never ends.

IN THE SCRIPTURES
1 Corinthians 13:4–13

> Love is patient; love is kind; love is not envious or boastful or arrogant or rude. It does not insist on it own way; it is not irritable or resentful; it does not rejoice in wrongdoing, but rejoices in the truth. It bears all things, believes all things, hopes all things, endures all things.
>
> Love never ends. But as for prophecies, they will come to an end; as for tongues, they will cease; as for knowledge, it will come to an end. For we know only in part, and we prophesy only in part; but when the complete comes, the partial will come to an end. When I was a child, I spoke like a child, I thought like a child, I reasoned like a child; when I became an adult, I put an end to childish ways. For now we see in a mirror, dimly, but then we will see face to face. Now I know only in part; then I will know fully, even as I have been fully known. And now faith, hope, and love abide, these three; and the greatest of these is love.

Paul lifts up love as the preeminent gift. He outlines the qualities of love and professes that love is the only gift that will last forever. The letter is in response to debate within Paul's community as to which is the greatest gift. Charismatic gifts such as speaking in tongues or prophecy are good and may be helpful to the community, but the community will not survive if it lacks love.

God's unconditional love can be a difficult thing for us to accept. Something about love makes us believe that it should not be free, should not be unconditional. When we are around young children we can get a tremendous insight into what unconditional love is. Children cannot survive alone; they need adult care. When they cry, we respond to them. We care for them until they are capable of caring for themselves. We never put limits on our love and care for young children. If we think of ourselves as young children before God, we can draw closer in understanding God's unconditional love. When we are hungry, God feeds us. When we need our diapers changed, God changes them. We would not refuse children their basic needs, and in the same way, God does not refuse us our basic needs.

Examining our unconditional love for the children in our lives, we soon discover that our love for them often springs from the fact that they are related to us. We might not so easily love other people's children the way we love our own.

Let this Advent be a time to practice loving others. How different the world would be if we loved all people, if we loved one another as ourselves. Loving one another means to lay down our lives for each other, as the Child explained to those who would follow him. Laying down our lives for others requires that we move from a place of self-protection to a place of self-giving. Love, as a concept, gets tossed around so easily. It rolls off our tongues quickly, usually having little or nothing to do with sacrifice, let alone offering our very lives. But those devoted to the project and mission of love know how much it can require our blood, sweat, and tears. Laughter and celebration do not tell the full story of love. Somehow, our love as Christians leads to and from the cross. Being at the foot of the cross gives us a unique understanding of the power of love. We see the suffering Christ and understand the price that love pays. As we journey through life and come upon the hard knocks of life and love, we would do well to return to the cross and spend time with the One who knows the price of love.

To see Christ suffering is to see and understand ourselves on the journey to love. In the same way, to see and touch the suffering of others is to understand the ongoing mission of Christ in the world today. Love for us does not exist without the compass of the cross. Wherever we experience suffering, our own or that of others, only the cross can orient us to the direction we must take. The cross is not easy; love is not easy. Yet we cannot have one without the other. What would our life be like if we wanted to experience the full power of love expressed in the cross? If love never ends, then the cross never ends. The cross and love are one. I wonder if Mary pondered this in her heart as she strove to stay open to God's will for her.

IN THE WOMB

Most of the Child's vernix—the creamy protective substance covering his body—has fallen off, revealing new skin beneath. His skin is actually quite sensitive, scaly and not smooth. Becoming a new creation always requires that we let go of the things we normally rely on to protect us and allow our new skin to be revealed.

During the fourth month of our pregnancy, I went with Kathy to the doctor. I remember trying to understand the image he kept showing me on the ultrasound's monitor. "There is his heart and there are his legs." I confess that I could never make out what the doctor was showing me.

Mary did not have the option of seeing Jesus in the womb, and yet she felt intimately connected the Child she could not see. Imagine how much of her trust she puts in God, whom she also cannot see. Soon Mary will join millions of mothers who see their babies for the first time and think them beautiful and perfect.

Sometimes when we undergo difficult experiences, it is easy for us to go back to the familiar, protective coverings that we used to avoid pain in the past. In difficult moments, we are called to focus on the power of God that is greater than the moments when we feel most desolate, afraid, and over-whelmed. Again, paying attention to our feelings helps us make the correct choices about what we do when we are in pain. Knowing our temptations, knowing our addictions, may well give us the strength to make new choices. Sometimes praying for a new experience of God's gift can help us move toward a new experience of loving ourselves, our neighbors, and God.

SPIRITUAL EXERCISE

Reread the passage from 1 Corinthians. Close your eyes and imagine the darkness of the womb. Try to imagine how the Child must look and feel at this stage of his development. Imagine that you are in a dark room. Be as still as possible.

Imagine that the Child comes to you, bringing you a candle and asking to sit with you. As he sits, he asks you about your heart. He repeats the question, "How is your heart?" Bring to mind the places and things where you might be experiencing hurt. As you think about these things, put your hand in the Child's hand. Slowly raise your hand to your heart and ask the Child to fill you with unconditional love for yourself and your life story. "Lord, clothe me in your loving-kindness," or "Lord, teach me to let go of past hurts."

For Today

❋ How can this Advent be a time for understanding the birth of the Child in the light of the cross?

❋ Ask God for the gift of love and the ability to forgive those who have hurt you.

❋ Remember that God is love and calls you to grow in love.

Advent 4: Wednesday

O come, O come Emmanuel,
and fulfill your promises in me today.

Advent is a time for us to receive the Holy Spirit, a time to experience God, and a time to obey the wishes of God.

IN THE SCRIPTURES
Matthew 1:18–25

> Now the birth of Jesus the Messiah took place in this way. When his mother Mary had been engaged to Joseph, but before they lived together, she was found to be with child from the Holy Spirit. Her husband Joseph, being a right-eous man and unwilling to expose her to public disgrace, planned to dismiss her quietly. But just when he had resolved to do this, an angel of the Lord appeared to him in a dream and said, "Joseph, son of David, do not be afraid to take Mary as your wife, for the child conceived in her is from the Holy Spirit. She will bear a son, and you are to name him Jesus, for he will save his people from their sins." All this took place to what had been spoken by the Lord through the prophet:
> "Look, the virgin shall conceive and bear a son,
>   and they shall name him Emmanuel,"
> which means, "God is with us." When Joseph awoke from sleep, he did as the angel of the Lord commanded him; he took her as his wife, but had no marital relations with her until she had borne a son; and he named him Jesus.

Matthew does not give us a scene in which Mary encounters an angel, but instead says she "was found to be with child from the Holy Spirit." Joseph decides to divorce Mary, but is warned in a dream that this child is the Savior received from the Holy Spirit. Joseph obeys the angel and takes Mary as his wife.

In most of the resurrection narratives, Jesus offers the disciples the gift of the Holy Spirit. We are a post-resurrection people, continuing to be blessed by the gift of the Holy Spirit. Most of us rarely give much thought to the Holy Spirit on a daily basis. If truth be told, many of us are a little puzzled about the role of the Holy Spirit. We hear mention of the Spirit in church, during baptisms, in prayers and blessings, when we make the sign of the cross. But most of us pay little attention to what the Spirit has to do with us personally.

If we spend time reflecting on the role of the Holy Spirit in our lives, we may discover many wonderful and exciting things. It is the Spirit who gives us life, spiritually and physically. We may shy away from dramatic expressions of the Spirit in our lives, but we can notice the more subtle signs. What does it mean to be filled with the Spirit? What does it mean to receive the Holy Spirit? What would it mean to be guided by the Holy Spirit this Advent? What did you notice about the Spirit alive in you today?

For Christians there is no spirituality apart from the Holy Spirit. We do not journey with crystals or cards; we journey with the Holy Spirit. And if something is of the Holy Spirit, it always gives birth to the Child. It is the Holy Spirit who leads us to Christmas. We journey not with baggage and gifts, but with and by the Holy Spirit. When we are guided by the Holy Spirit, we always arrive at the right place.

Only the Holy Spirit can lead us to Christ and to community, and this is why it is so important that during Advent we seek to be filled with the Holy Spirit. Mary allowed herself to be so filled. We sometimes overlook how confusing this period must have been for Mary and Joseph. They must have felt they were in over their heads, filled with worries, doubts, uncertainties, fear, and wonder. How does a teenager say to her husband-to-be that she is pregnant? How does a man break off an engagement? How do parents trust that having a child is a good and wise thing?

Matthew does not show the angel visiting Mary in his version of the nativity story. Many times when our lives are disturbed and turned upside down, there are no signs, signals, or warning. Disease, death, failure, and pain can sneak up on us. It is never easy to experience God in surprises like these. We naturally prefer pleasant experiences of life in God. Quite frequently, however, God comes to us in a sudden turn of events in life. How can we grow in our trust of God at times like these? How do we cultivate receptivity to God in all our life experiences? Can we surrender and accept that painful moments can also offer precious experiences of God's saving love?

In Advent we nurture a desire to respond to God's call to turn the other cheek. Love your enemies. Do good to those who hate you. Serve one another. Take up the cross. Follow me. Deny yourself. Believe in God. Come and see. Feed my sheep. Do this in memory of me. Make disciples. Give them something to eat. Love God with your whole heart. Go sell what you have and give the money to the poor. Give to God the things that are God's. Stay awake. Yes, the Child, too, has a shopping list. What would it be like to give the Child one of his wishes for Christmas?

IN THE WOMB

 The Child's brain is still growing; growth is still happening in small and necessary ways. As the brain grows there are five main bony plates in the skull that will play an important role at the time of delivery. These plates will provide the Child's skull with flexibility in order to ease delivery. His skull will need to change shape in order for him to be born. Mary feels the physical shift of the Child as he settles down lower in the abdomen in preparation for birth. As the head falls more firmly and decidedly into place, it brings to mind Jesus' turning toward Jerusalem during his last days on earth. Have you ever wondered about Mary's state of mind at this time? What was in Mary's head—what was she thinking—just days before giving birth?

We often take a rigid view toward many of our life projects. We think we cannot be born without an unbending will. Quite frequently, God comes to us and asks us to relax and let go. Can we trust God to reshape our hard heads? The thoughts we hold determine the spiritual shape and flexibility of our entire lives. When was the last time we sought to change an idea or approach to something that had long since ceased to bear fruit for us, simply because we had gotten into a familiar rut? Christmas is near. Now is the time.

SPIRITUAL EXERCISE

Reread the passage from Matthew. Close your eyes and imagine the darkness of the womb. Try to imagine how the Child must look and feel at this stage of his development. Imagine that you paid Mary a visit shortly after she discovered that she was pregnant. What would you say to her?

Then imagine that you got another chance to visit her shortly before she gives birth. How does she look different from the first time? What would you say to her now? Ask her to tell you something to help you on your spiritual journey. Listen to what she says. Say, "Lord, create in me a new mind."

For Today

   ❋ How can this Advent be a time of renewed perspectives for the spiritual life?
   ❋ Ask God for the gift of discernment and the ability to be compassionate.
   ❋ Pray for the grace to know that God's ways are often not our ways.

Advent 4: Thursday

O come, O come Emmanuel,
and be known to me today.

Advent is a time to focus on knowing God, to meditate on
the incarnation, and to humble ourselves before God.

IN THE SCRIPTURES
Philippians 2:1–11

If then there is any encouragement in Christ, any consola-
tion from love, any sharing in the Spirit, any compassion
and sympathy, make my joy complete: be of the same
mind, having the same love, being in full accord and of
one mind. Do nothing from selfish ambition or conceit,
but in humility regard others as better than yourselves. Let
each of you look not to your own interests, but to the
interests of others. Let the same mind be in you that was in
Christ Jesus,
    who, though he was in the form of God,
    did not regard equality with God
      as something to be exploited,
    but emptied himself, taking the form of a slave,
      being born in human likeness.
And being found in human form, he humbled himself
    and became obedient to the point of death—
      even death on a cross.
Therefore God also highly exalted him
    and gave him the name that is above every name,
so that at the name of Jesus every knee should bend,
    in heaven and on earth and under the earth,
    and every tongue should confess

that Jesus Christ is Lord,
to the glory of God the Father.

This passage from Philippians includes one of the earliest Christian hymns, sung by the early Christians during their worship. In the hymn, these Christians profess their understanding of God's love as expressed through the divine act of the incarnation. Themes of service and humility underscore their understanding of the Child and what the Christian life demands from them as believers.

Advent is nearly over. Throughout Advent we have been meditating on the "surpassing value of knowing Christ Jesus my Lord" (Philippians 3:8). In the birth of God as human, we see God's tremendous love for all humanity. We look to Christmas to understand God's activity in the world because, indeed, the birth and life of the Child point to God's creation and mission.

Like any kind of knowledge, knowledge of the Child is never-ending. How wonderful it would be if this Advent has deepened our knowledge and understanding of God! To make God our one desire demands of us that we focus on God and the things of God. St. Paul writes repeatedly that he considers everything as rubbish compared to the value of knowing of God.

This kind of focus requires discipline. Today, we tend to have difficulties with the word "discipline." Interestingly, it shares the same root as the word "disciple." To focus on God in a disciplined way is to follow God. To follow God is to seek to know God as the disciple seeks to know the master. To know God is our vocation.

And so we meditate on the incarnation during Advent. Who can explain the mystery of God incarnate? Many have tried, but until we dive into the mystery of it and experience it fully, we will never understand it. God becoming human is the offer for all humanity to become God. The more we understand the gift of life, the more we can understand the incarnation. Noticing the joyous moments in our lives, we get an insight into the joy of what it means to be human. Our creativity and our ability to form life-giving relationships speak to the nature of the Child.

Those who are poor and those who suffer teach us about the incarnate God because they bear the marks of God. The hungry and thirsty, the prisoner, the depressed, the lost, and the stranger teach us who God is. Did not God come as a poor child into an insignificant town? Did God not die on a shameful cross? Looking to the heavens, looking to glorious things is not where we find the incarnation. We experience God incarnate in the "daily-ness" of life and in the people and situations where we least expect to find God. To know the incarnation is to go beyond our comfort zones to the margins because, after all, that is what the Child did.

Advent is a time to humble ourselves before God. *Human—humus—humility.* During Lent we hear, "Remember that you are dust." It is amazing how we go through extremes to prove that we are not dust. In being humble, we are not called to grovel and make ourselves any worse than we are. But humility does call us to accept that we are all God's children and that God is the author of life.

We are all created by God; we are all God's children. Whenever we hear ourselves speaking of "those people," we should ask ourselves, Who do we think we are? Behind the smokescreen of inclusiveness, the privileged only grow more exclusive. Behind the façade of compassion, many have grown more merciless. Beneath the tolerance, we are becoming more intolerant. Know this: Our harsh ways of dealing with self and others come from a lack of humility before God. If we could see ourselves as servants of God, we would order our lives differently. It is in obedience that humility is purified.

IN THE WOMB

 All of the Child's organs are developed, though he will not have any teeth for several months. It is a small detail, but a powerful reminder of his humanity. He comes in peace, after all; he is heralded as the Prince of Peace. There is no bite to him.

I can still remember watching helplessly as my mother went off to the hospital to give birth to my younger brother. I also watched helplessly as my wife went into labor; all I could do was to trust that my presence next to her and my love for her during the previous nine months would help to ease the pain in some way. But I also noticed that she was helpless in the face of her body's reaction: her pain, her cries, her tears, and her desire for the pain to pass.

The Child has no teeth. Mary is far away from home, but she has her faith, she has her husband, and she has her child. All three of them wait and get ready.

SPIRITUAL EXERCISE

Reread the passage from Philippians. Close your eyes and imagine the darkness of the womb. Try to imagine how the Child must look and feel at this stage of his development.

Now imagine you are journeying with Mary and Joseph as the time of birth approaches. It is night, and you all stop to take a rest. What does it feel like to be journeying with them? What do you notice about Mary? How can you offer to help? Say, "Lord, let me be present in the midst of her pain."

For Today

* How can this Advent be a time of renewed love in your life?
* Ask God for the gift to see all those you encounter as the Child incarnate.
* Remember that God calls us to love one another as we are loved by God.

Advent 4: Friday

O come, O come Emmanuel,
and give me your good news today.

Advent is a time to hear the good news that God has offered salvation to all.

IN THE SCRIPTURES
Luke 2:8–12

> In that region there were shepherds living in the fields, keeping watch over their flock by night. Then an angel of the Lord stood before them, and the glory of the Lord shone around them, and they were terrified. But the angel said to them, "Do not be afraid; for see—I am bringing you good news of great joy for all people: to you is born this day in the city of David a Savior, who is the Messiah, the Lord. This will be a sign for you: you will find a child wrapped in bands of cloth and lying in a manger."

A frightening light shines down on the shepherds as they receive the good news of the Child's birth. Shepherds did not hold an honorable place in Hebrew society. Because of their duties with the sheep, they were considered outcasts and unclean. Once again, we are called to solidarity with those ignored by the powerful in society. Who are the people we do not associate with in our daily comings and goings? Who are the present-day shepherds in our society? How do we connect to people out in the fields? Can we intercede on their behalf for justice and access to social goods?

When we think of this part of the nativity story, we also think back to the story of David and his day of anointing. He was out tending the sheep, virtually ignored, while his seven brothers were inside hosting Samuel. As soon as Samuel saw David, he recognized him as the chosen one. Similarly, the shepherds are chosen as recipients of the angel's good news of the Child's birth.

In what remains of this season of Advent, with Christmas fast approaching, we would do well to remember how God continues to bring good news to the poor and those on the margins. Moreover, those aspects of our lives that we leave out or ignore or deny are the very places where God chooses to shine a light and offer good news.

It is strange that while Advent is joyous, it is also a penitential time, a time to reflect on the ways that we have not heard or embodied the good news. The shepherds were terrified by God's light and wonders. We are sometimes terrified by the ways we obscure and obfuscate God's presence. In either case, God seeks to encourage us, though we are not encouraged to stay safe and keep on doing what we are doing. Instead, God calls us to make a journey. The journey that children make as pageant-shepherds in our well-cleaned churches is not the journey we are called to make. We are called to journey in a way that resembles the birth pangs of a mother in labor. We are called to climb mountains of love, brave rivers that seek to drown us, face the heat and the cold—all the time believing that the God who called us will sustain us and reward us with new life.

The joy and love of Advent and Christmas are authenticated only in following the Child. In following we seek always to encounter Christ on the way and at the journey's end.

IN THE WOMB

From his mother the Child receives a temporary supply of natural antibodies to protect him from viruses and sicknesses that can cause illness in newborns. The mission of Mary's womb is nearly accomplished. It is almost time to expel the Child from the womb. Hormones are already at work to initiate labor cramps. Mary's muscles have been contracting. She is experiencing very serious pain. But from somewhere deep within her, faith assures her, because the faith of her elders was this: God will take care of you.

Growing up in Jamaica, I heard people singing this song as long as I could remember: "God will take care of you." I am sure Mary must have felt this from the moment of the Annunciation. Once she had said *yes* to God, God had provided for her and been with her in a deeper way. Of course things got difficult and scary, but Mary must have grown to trust God, as she saw the workings of God in the lives of Joseph, Zechariah, and Elizabeth.

God took care of Mary and she must have felt the power of his care demonstrated in and through the Child growing in her womb. God also took special care of the Child, all the way to the end, the end of his time in the womb, and the end of his time on earth.

SPIRITUAL EXERCISE

Reread the passage from Luke. Close your eyes and imagine the darkness of the womb. Try to imagine how the Child must look and feel at this stage of his development. As you imagine how the Child responds to the contractions of the womb, think of your own labor pains (physical or emotional) or those of someone you love. If you have not had this experience, think of a time when you were in tremendous pain and how its passing eventually led to a time of joy or celebration.

Now think of a friend or a stranger who may be going through a difficult time right now. Imagine that you are an angel of mercy, consoling and being present to this person. Say, "Lord, teach me to think of those who are suffering at this time."

For Today

* How do the remaining hours of Advent offer a more
urgent call to be present to the joys and suffering of
others?

* Ask God for the gift to see that suffering can be
redemptive, even the needless suffering that can be
avoided through compassionate intervention.

* Remember that God calls us to bear each other's burdens.

Advent 4: Saturday

O come, O come Emmanuel,
and lead me to Bethlehem today.

Advent is a time of urgency, a time to make haste to open
our eyes to what God has done.

IN THE SCRIPTURES
Luke 2:13–16

And suddenly there was with the angel a multitude of the
heavenly host, praising God and saying,
   "Glory to God in the highest heaven,
      and on earth peace among those whom he favors!"
When the angels had left them and gone into heaven, the
shepherds said to one another, "Let us go now to
Bethlehem and see this thing that has taken place, which
the Lord has made known to us." So they went with haste
and found Mary and Joseph, and the child lying in a
manger.

The shepherds who hear of the birth of the Child make haste
to see what the angel told them. Notice how the shepherds
decide to go together, and quickly.

Advent is a time to make spiritual haste. "Let us go now," the shepherds say. It is never too late to set out to see Christ. The announcement of the birth to the shepherds came after the Child was born. In the same way, the invitation comes to us today. The Child is born, the promise is fulfilled: we need to go and take part in the ongoing story.

As Christians, we need to bring a certain urgency to how we live out our Christian values. Our urgency comes from a place of love: we are called to go see the helpless, newborn child. The Child, who resembles the weak among us, invites all of us to come and see him—and to see ourselves in him. Where do we encounter weakness in our own hearts? How do we become a neighbor to those who are weak in our society? How well do we represent the visiting and caring presence of God in the world?

When we live lives characterized by love and caring, we model who God is in the world today. Church communities that take seriously their call to model God's reign offer what secular institutions cannot: devotion to the ideal of unmerited love and care, conscious effort to avoid evil, and an ideal of fruitfulness in which gain is understood through sharing. Following Jesus' way of life, Christians have a school in which to live differently and better.

Strangely enough, we cannot model a better way of living without first encountering God. Many hear and see the angels, but choose to stay out in the fields. Advent calls us to respond differently. Advent calls us to be outstanding in our field, as opposed to be out standing in the field. To be outstanding in the field is to detach from the things and ways that are not of God and to stand with God.

Today is the day when we need to leave the things that keep us busy to go and see. God has come to us. The time has come. Let us go in haste. Let us go today.

IN THE WOMB

Just as the Child's hormones and antibodies prepare the Child for life in the world, his mother will call upon similar hormones as well as all her physical strength to deliver him. The mission of Mary's womb is almost completed, and Mary is going through the painful stages of laboring to push the Child through the birth canal.

Only a woman knows how to read her body in these crucial moments. She who has watched her womb grow and hold the Child knows that the womb will tell her without a doubt when the birth will take place. Labor takes its time—nothing will happen before the right time.

It has been nine months, and now the end is near. The womb that has held the baby Jesus is ready to give him up.

Up to this point the womb has been a safe, calm, and gentle container, but now it must do what it has to do, and so it begins to contract, causing Mary much pain and probably some discomfort and confusion or even alarm for the Child. Labor has begun.

With the breaking of the water, Mary knows that her Child will be born soon. This water, a mixture of amniotic and other body fluids, is the first in a series of signs that birth is imminent. She feels the slow but persistent labor pains and struggles to stay clear and calm as they increase in speed and frequency.

Birth is never painless, easy, neat, or simple. Yet the womb continues its relentless work, despite the discomfort of the Child or the agony of the mother—and such is the way of life. It is in these moments that a woman must trust her body, which intuitively knows that pain will give way to life and joy. Perhaps in between her contractions Mary took strength in the psalms: "Weeping may linger for the night, but joy comes with the morning" (30:5).

SPIRITUAL EXERCISE

Reread the passage from Luke. Close your eyes and imagine the darkness of the womb. Try to imagine how the Child must look and feel at this stage of his development. Picture yourself in the room where the Child is about to be born. Notice the animals and any people present. Look closely at Mary's face as she surrenders to the labor pains. What is it that Mary and Joseph will ask of you as they get ready to give birth? Say, "Lord, teach me to be loving and kind."

For Today

※ How are you called to be faithful in and through the hardships of life?

※ Ask God to increase within you the gift of perseverance and faithfulness.

※ Remember that "weeping may linger for the night, but joy comes with the morning."

Christmas Day

THE FEAST
OF THE
INCARNATION

O come, O come Emmanuel,
and be born in us today.

The Christ Child is born, amid joy, worship, and danger.

IN THE SCRIPTURES
Matthew 2:1–3, 9–12

In the time of King Herod, after Jesus was born in
Bethlehem of Judea, wise men from the East came to
Jerusalem, asking, Where is the child who has been born
king of the Jews? For we observed his star at its rising, and
have come to pay him homage.".. .

When they had heard the king, they set out; and there,
ahead of them, went the star that they had seen at its rising, until it stopped over the place where the child was.
When they saw that the star had stopped, they were overwhelmed with joy. On entering the house, they saw the
child with Mary his mother; and they knelt down and paid
him homage. Then, opening their treasure chests, they
offered him gifts of gold, frankincense, and myrrh. And
having been warned in a dream not to return to Herod,
they left for their own country by another road.

Notice the word *wise* in this passage from Matthew's gospel. It is those who are wise who come to Jerusalem. They come seeking the child. Even with their wisdom they still need to ask, "Where is the child?"

On so many levels, the journey of the magi captures our experience of Christmas. We too are on a journey, a journey that will lead us through and beyond the palaces of Herod to a place of new life, a place where life is vulnerable, a place where we are "overwhelmed with joy."

What can we learn from those who were described as wise? They were willing to follow a star—a reminder that the answers we seek quite frequently lie beyond us. Sometimes we do have to look out, look up, and look beyond ourselves. This is a powerful message of Advent: we are called to make a journey to Jerusalem, the city of peace, knowing that at the end of our journey we will find the Prince of Peace.

When wisdom leads us to seek God, the result is always joy: "When they saw that the star had stopped, they were overwhelmed with joy." Yet wisdom and joy are not enough; we must enter the house where the Child is. We must see the Child, must kneel down and pay him homage. We must give of ourselves. After all this is done, we can never return to life as it was before.

What joy to behold. What joy to the world. What joy for you and me.

IN THE WOMB

 Mary has endured the labor pains and is now working hard to push the Child out into the world. The first phase of Mary's mission of motherhood is now accomplished. Now the Child is free; he gulps and gasps, inhaling the breath of God. With a loud scream, a new journey has begun. The Child is born. He has arrived safe and sound into the loving family of Mary and Joseph. The mother looks into his beautiful face; he tilts his head toward her. Their eyes embrace.

Years ago my wife and I discussed how to help the children understand the power of Christmas and the gift of Jesus' birth. We decided on a manger containing a Christ Child doll and beside the Child's head, we placed a mirror. When the children and the parents approached the manger to look in, they saw not only the babe, but also themselves reflected— just as the newborn Child sees himself reflected in his mother's loving eyes and knows that he is good.

After all the pain, there is joy and rejoicing. It is a beautiful day. The Child, our Savior, has come to live among us. Rejoice. Rejoice. Rejoice. Alleluia!

SPIRITUAL EXERCISE

Reread the passage from Luke. Close your eyes and imagine that Mary has invited you to take up and hold the Child who has just been born. Hold him in your arms, tenderly. Look into his face. Smell his baby breath. Caress his velvety skin. Feel his tiny weight. Notice how full of possibility he is. As you hold him, call to mind your favorite Christmas carol and sing it to him as a lullaby. Say, "Thank you, God, for the gift of your Son, Jesus."

For Today
  ❊ Offer prayers of joy and gratitude for the gift of the Child.
  ❊ When you go to church, pay special attention to the readings and the preaching.
  ❊ Remember that the Child's birth is only the beginning of your adventures.

The womb is empty.
The world is full of possibility.